NEW HAVEN FREE

W9-AKD-995

35000095829668

OFFICIALLY WITHDRAWN
NEW HAVEN FREE PUBLIC LIBRARY

ISSUES IN CYBERSPACE
FROM PRIVACY TO PIRACY

COMPUTING AND CONNECTING IN THE 21ST CENTURY

ISSUES IN
CYBERSPACE
FROM PRIVACY TO PIRACY

EDITED BY ROBERT CURLEY, MANAGER, SCIENCE AND TECHNOLOGY

Britannica
Educational Publishing

IN ASSOCIATION WITH

ROSEN
EDUCATIONAL SERVICES

Published in 2012 by Britannica Educational Publishing
(a trademark of Encyclopædia Britannica, Inc.)
in association with Rosen Educational Services, LLC
29 East 21st Street, New York, NY 10010.

Copyright © 2012 Encyclopædia Britannica, Inc. Britannica, Encyclopædia Britannica, and the Thistle logo are registered trademarks of Encyclopædia Britannica, Inc. All rights reserved.

Rosen Educational Services materials copyright © 2012 Rosen Educational Services, LLC. All rights reserved.

Distributed exclusively by Rosen Educational Services.
For a listing of additional Britannica Educational Publishing titles, call toll free (800) 237-9932.

First Edition

Britannica Educational Publishing
Michael I. Levy: Executive Editor
J.E. Luebering: Senior Manager
Adam Augustyn: Assistant Manager, Encyclopædia Britannica
Marilyn L. Barton: Senior Coordinator, Production Control
Steven Bosco: Director, Editorial Technologies
Lisa S. Braucher: Senior Producer and Data Editor
Yvette Charboneau: Senior Copy Editor
Kathy Nakamura: Manager, Media Acquisition
Robert Curley: Manager, Science and Technology

Rosen Educational Services
Jeanne Nagle: Senior Editor
Nelson Sá: Art Director
Cindy Reiman: Photography Manager
Brian Garvey: Designer, Cover Design
Introduction by Heather M. Moore Niver

Library of Congress Cataloging-in-Publication Data

Issues in cyberspace: from privacy to piracy/edited by Robert Curley.—1st ed.
   p. cm.
"In association with Britannica Educational Publishing, Rosen Educational Services."
Includes bibliographical references and index.
ISBN 978-1-61530-693-0 (library binding)
1. Cyberspace. 2. Internet—Social aspects. I. Curley, Robert, 1955–
HM851.I68 2012
303.48'33—dc23

2011030767

Manufactured in the United States of America

Cover, pp. iii, 1, 20, 45, 61, 94, 128, 131, 137 Shutterstock.com; pp. iii, 4, 7, 8, 24, 50, 51, 68, 87, 88, 117, 118 © www.istockphoto.com/Andrey Volodin; pp. v, vi, vii (background graphic), ix © www.istockphoto.com/Simfo; pp. viii-ix © www.istockphoto.com/Axaulya; pp, 21, 34, 37, 66, 77, 91 © www.istockphoto.com/Karl Dolenc; remaining interior background image © www.istockphoto.com/Johan Ramberg

CONTENTS

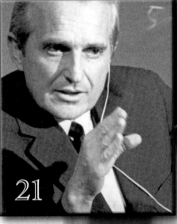

303.483 ISSUES
Issues in cyberspace :from
privacy to piracy /
35000095829668
MAIN LIBRARY

INTRODUCTION

In addition to living on planet Earth, a large part of the world's population also resides in a realm known as cyberspace. Cyberspace is a computer-mediated realm where people gather and exchange information, access entertainment, and keep up social contact, all with the click of a mouse. The course of modern life is a testament to the importance of cyberspace. In fewer than 50 years, the Internet has gone from being a relatively unknown entity, used by only a few programmers and scientists, to an essential part of daily life for more than 25 percent of the world's general population. Many people start their day by checking online news or weather sites, reading electronic mail (e-mail) messages, or logging in to a social networking site. Cell phones stream music or show the location of the nearest coffee shop with the touch of a screen. Some businesses, called e-businesses, do all their sales and service online.

With the public so globally connected through the cyberspace infrastructure, psychological, sociological, economic, and political issues have begun to arise. This book addresses the roots and growth of cyberspace in today's technology-oriented world, as well as the issues engendered by virtual communities.

ix

The road to cyberspace began in California's "Valley of the Heart's Delights," an area once thick with orchards. Into this valley of fruit-laden trees came an electrical engineer named Frederick E. Terman, a Stanford University professor who set out to bolster the university's electrical engineering department by investing in several communications start-up companies that were conducting cutting-edge research. Terman's creation, the Stanford Industrial Park, became a hotbed of electronic technology, with an emphasis on the manufacture and refinement of semiconductors. The region quickly became known as Silicon Valley—so named for silicon, which is the base material in computer semiconductors.

Advances in technology proceeded apace. In 1979 Apple Computer, Inc. (now Apple Inc.), created the Apple II, which was popular with schools and gamers, and two years later International Business Machines (IBM) produced the more "serious" personal computer (PC). The Valley grew and prospered throughout the 1980s and '90s, as the personal computer, software, and Internet-based businesses became increasingly popular.

While Silicon Valley was perfecting computer hardware and software, the United States military was helping to shape the channels of computer-based communication. The Defense Advanced Research Projects Agency (DARPA) created the ARPANET, a decentralized network designed to transfer copious amounts of data. The ARPANET is widely considered the forerunner of today's Internet.

At the same time, members of the 1960s-era counterculture living in and around Silicon Valley and the San Francisco Bay area expanded many online practices in an attempt to take computing out of establishment confines and make it more accessible to the masses. Among these computer revolutionaries was Stewart Brand, publisher of the Whole Earth Catalog, who kick-started the trend toward the electronic bulletin board system (BBS). Nowadays the BBS is a common way for people to exchange ideas about everything from music to medical practices, regardless of their location. Electronic mail (e-mail), instant messaging (IM), and short message service (SMS) text messaging also burgeoned as a means of personal communication, especially among young people. Social networking sites such as Facebook and the business-centred LinkedIn proliferated as well.

Utilizing cyberspace tools such as these, people around the world have become increasingly interconnected. Online communication has turned into a gateway to concrete action. Organized by means such as texting and IMs, groups called "flash mobs" have gathered groups of strangers to participate in light-hearted endeavours such as singing, dancing, or massive pillow fights. In recent years, however, flash mobs have begun to take on a more serious tone and political bent. For example, In January 2011, Egyptians used the electronic media in a call to demonstrate against their longtime leader, Pres. Hosni Mubarak.

One of the most prominent issues raised by the advent of cyberspace concerned the open-source movement. The question of whether or not to share programming code has been debated since the 1960s. At that time the computing counterculture had determined that control over the Internet should be decentralized. Subsequently, computer programmers started to work toward openly sharing information related to source codes. (In contrast, proponents of the closed-source model believe such codes should be kept by the individuals or companies who invented them, in order to protect copyright and income.)

Developers of the UNIX operating system were among the first to successfully and reliably share code.

One of the advantages to sharing code was that programs could be regularly improved and updated. Bugs and quirks could be smoothed out frequently, even daily. In 1991, the Linux platform, created by a 21-year-old computer scientist from Finland, became the first major open-source project based on the Internet. The advantages to Linux were that it crashed infrequently and, because it was an open-source product, it could be adapted for different uses.

Cloud computing, which refers to software applications that are run and stored on the Internet, is a growing part of cyberspace. Cloud computing can be used in many different ways: to run discrete software applications, process and store information remotely, and combine software and hardware capabilities within the framework of a remote platform. All kinds of businesses and services, from social network sites to major software companies to companies that sell e-books, music files, and cell-phone apps, are moving into "the cloud."

The same openness that allows for easy communication and file sharing is not without its vulnerabilities. Privacy is a chief concern in cyberspace, primarily because there are a number of ways to monitor the use of computers, cell phones, and other cyberspace technology. "Cookies," which are electronic files that track a user's Internet activity, are easily placed on a computer. They can show what an individual searches for and reads online, and even how long a person spends on a particular site. The fear is that some cookies are also able to gather logins, passwords, and other personal data. "Geotags," which are bits of location data embedded in photographic images, are another potential threat to personal privacy.

Data mining—discovering patterns and relationships in the way people access and move massive amounts of data—can be useful in business and science research,

Unfortunately, collecting data also borders on intrusion when the data contain personal information such as medical records or telephone bills. Certainly, not all such data collection is used for nefarious purposes, but this precisely recorded information can be dangerous if it gets into the wrong hands.

Sadly, with almost every technological advance comes a new potential for crime. Individuals, corporations, and even governments have been the victims of criminals who might be anywhere in the world and can take cover almost anywhere. A disturbing lack of international cybercrime treaties complicates matters and makes apprehension of cybercriminals very difficult.

Cybercriminals are individuals who use the Internet to put a new spin on crimes that have existed for years: fraud, child pornography, and music pirating, for instance. Identity theft in particular is a cybercrime on the rise. Identity thieves access personal information that users register on Web sites or gain access to a person's computer files. Armed with only a credit card number and a name, cybercriminals can run up enormous bills and ruin a person's credit.

Hacking is the act of illegally gaining access to computers or networks, often for no other reason than to wreak havoc. Some hackers merely enjoy the challenge of breaking into computers. But cybercrime can extend beyond inconveniencing businesses and PC users, even becoming a national security issue. In 1981, 17-year-old Kevin Mitnick allegedly broke into the North American Aerospace Defense Command (NORAD) computers, a feat that landed him on the U.S. Federal Bureau of Investigation's "most wanted" list. Web sites are also vulnerable to hacking. On July 4, 2011, the FoxNews.com Twitter feed was hacked, sending out erroneous messages that U.S. Pres. Barack Obama had been assassinated.

"Malware" (an abbreviation for "malicious software") infects computers through viruses, trojans, or worms attached to e-mail messages or embedded in Web sites or operating systems. These entities can take over a computer and turn it into a zombie—meaning a computer that doesn't behave normally and is under the control of the malware perpetrator. Infected computers are often part of a "botnet" (network of zombie computers) used to circulate illicit software. Another malware tactic is the denial-of-service attack. This is an assault on commercial or government Web sites, wherein botnet computers flood a server with so many requests for activity or information that they overwhelm the system and shuts down the Web site.

Piracy is another hot-button issue in cyberspace. This involves downloading, copying, and distributing copyrighted music, movies, and text. In 2001, the file-sharing Web site Napster came under fire for what is known as peer-to-peer sharing of compressed music files called MP3s on their site. Individual purchasers argued that it was within the realm of fair use to listen to and share their purchased music however and wherever they liked. The Recording Industry Association of America (RIAA), however, argued that sharing files of copyrighted music with thousands of others went beyond fair use and was "digital piracy."

Following in the footsteps of the RIAA, the Motion Picture Association of America also has fought against piracy and bootlegging of movies. Meanwhile, the popularity of e-book readers has brought publishing fully into the digital age. Authors and publishers generally take defensive measures against e-book piracy by integrating digital rights management software into their products that limits the use of titles distributed electronically.

Another trend in cyberspace, media convergence, makes it difficult to control creative content, however. Newspapers, magazines, recordings, radio, television, films, and entertainment software are all interconnected in cyberspace through the possibility (and, in this day and age, high probability) of electronic dissemination.

Media convergence has been seen as a boon by some and a scourge by others. On the plus side, electronic distribution via computers and hand-held devices can boost a content provider's bottom line either by offering content for a direct fee or simply by driving traffic to related revenue-producing streams. The downside is that many content producers are wary of providing e-versions of their creations for fear that doing so will encourage piracy or otherwise undercut their rights to the product.

The worldwide popularity of the Internet certainly has meant an increase in electronic commerce (e-commerce). Yet rather than serving strictly as a place where users are merely consumers of information and goods, cyberspace also is considered a space for collaboration—a state fondly referred to as Web 2.0. Sites such as Flickr and YouTube, which allow users to post and view photographs and videos online, as well as social networking sites such as Facebook and Match.com, are indicative of the Web 2.0 culture; they are designed to foster interaction and connect individual users. Blogs, which are basically online personal journals, invite comments from readers. People with no formal training in reportage have been transformed into "citizen journalists" when they have recorded and posted newsworthy events online. Students can participate in online lessons and classes from anywhere in the world through distance learning.

The Internet has made it possible for people all over the world to communicate, play games, and even create virtual communities and economies. The explosion of the Internet's popularity also has brought concerns over privacy and computer safety to a new level. None of the many cyberspace issues should be taken lightly. But with vigilance, common sense, and a sense of social responsibility on the part of the user, there is little reason for users not to sit back and enjoy—and benefit from—the rich variety of content that abounds in cyberspace.

CHAPTER 1

A NEW WORLD

The Internet, technically a system architecture that allows computer networks around the world to interconnect in a sort of "network of networks," emerged in the United States in the 1970s but did not become visible to the general public until the early 1990s. Originally limited to a small, enclosed universe of programmers and scientific users, it quickly has become one of the world's most important communications media.

At the beginning of the 21st century, approximately 360 million people, or roughly 6 percent of the world's population, were estimated to have access to the Internet. By 2010 that number had grown to almost 2 billion, or more than 25 percent of the world's population. More than 68 percent of American households have connections to the Internet, and much of Europe is even better connected. Some 70 percent of households in the European Union are online, with Internet access reaching 90 percent of households in the Netherlands and Luxembourg and more than 80 percent in Sweden and Denmark. South Korea is the world leader in connecting its population to the Internet through high-speed broadband connections—more than 90 percent of all households.

Such statistics can chart the Internet's growth, but they offer few insights into the changes wrought as users—individuals, groups, corporations, and governments—have embedded the technology into everyday life. The Internet provides a capability so powerful and general that it can

Members of a South Korean family connect to the Internet. South Korea has the highest percentage of households with high-speed broadband access to the Web. Chung Sung-Jun/Getty Images

be used for almost any purpose that depends on information, and it is accessible by every individual who connects to one of its constituent networks. It supports human communication via electronic mail (e-mail), "chat rooms," newsgroups, social and gaming networks, and audio and video streaming, allowing people to work collaboratively at many different locations.

The Internet has dramatically transformed business as well as society. It has proved to be a spawning ground for a large and growing number of "e-businesses" (including subsidiaries of traditional "brick-and-mortar" companies) that carry out most of their sales and services online.

THE VALLEY OF THE HEART'S DELIGHTS

To understand the origins, complexity, and transformative power of the Internet, it is useful to study Silicon Valley, an industrial region around the southern shores of San Francisco Bay in California. Silicon Valley is bounded by the Santa Cruz Mountains on the west and the Diablo Range on the east, and has its intellectual centre at Palo Alto, home of Stanford University.

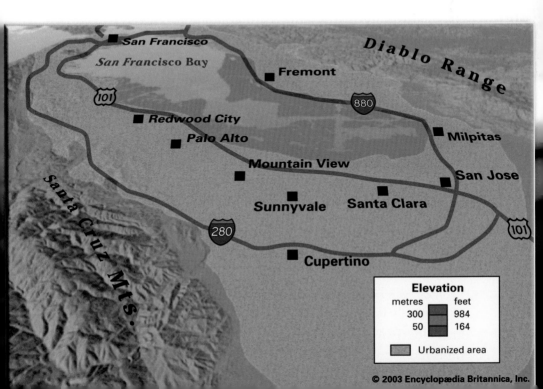

Elevation

metres		feet
300		984
50		164

Urbanized area

© 2003 Encyclopædia Britannica, Inc.

SEMICONDUCTORS

Semiconductors are crystalline solids intermediate in electrical conductivity between a conductor and an insulator. Semiconductors are employed in the manufacture of various kinds of electronic devices, including diodes, transistors, and integrated circuits. Such devices have found wide application because of their compactness, reliability, power efficiency, and low cost. As discrete components, they have found use in power devices, optical sensors, and light emitters, including solid-state lasers. They have a wide range of current- and voltage-handling capabilities and, more important, lend themselves to integration into complex but readily manufacturable microelectronic circuits. They are, and will be in the foreseeable future, the key elements for the majority of electronic systems, serving communications, signal processing, computing, and control applications in both the consumer and industrial markets.

Early in the 20th century the area was a bucolic region dominated by agriculture and known as the "Valley of the Heart's Delights," owing to the popularity of the fruits grown in its orchards. Today the region is known for the dense concentration of electronics and computer companies that have sprung up there since the mid-20th century. Silicon is the base material of the semiconductors employed in computer circuits, hence the name "Silicon Valley."

But Silicon Valley is not only a geographic location. The very name is synonymous with the rise of the computer and electronics industry as well as the emergence of the digital economy and the Internet. As such, Silicon Valley is also a state of mind, an idea about regional economic development, and part of a new mythology of American wealth. Other U.S. states and even other countries have attempted to create their own "Silicon Valleys," but they

Frederick E. Terman is considered a founding father of what is known today as Silicon Valley. [Frederick E. Terman]. Stanford Historical Photograph Collection (SHPC). Dept. of Special Collections and University Archives, Stanford University Libraries, Stanford, CA.

have often failed to re-create elements that were crucial to the success of the original.

FROM ORCHARDS TO INDUSTRIAL PARKS

If any single person is responsible for Silicon Valley, it is the electrical engineer and administrator Frederick E. Terman (1900–82). While a graduate student at the Massachusetts Institute of Technology (MIT; Ph.D., 1924), Terman saw how the faculty at Cambridge actively pursued research, as well as contact with industry through consulting and the placement of students in corporations. Returning home to Palo Alto in 1925 to join the faculty at Stanford, where he had received his undergraduate degree, Terman realized that Stanford's electrical engineering department was deficient. At MIT the faculty were experts in a broad range of fields—electronics, power engineering, computing, and communications—all on the leading edge of research. At Stanford the electrical engineering department had a single focus—electric power engineering.

Terman set out to build Stanford into a major centre of radio and communications research. He also encouraged students such as William Hewlett and David Packard (of the Hewlett-Packard Co.) and Eugene Litton (of Litton Industries, Inc.) to establish local companies. Terman invested in these "start-up" enterprises, personally demonstrating his desire to integrate the university with industry in the region.

When the United States entered World War II in 1941, Terman was made director of Harvard University's Radio Research Laboratory, which was dedicated to producing radar-jamming and other electronic-countermeasure technologies. At war's end he returned to Stanford as dean of engineering, intent on transforming Stanford into a West Coast MIT. First, he selected technologies for research emphasis; given his wartime work on microwave radar, he began with microwave electronics. Second, he solicited military contracts to fund academic research by faculty members who had worked in microwave technology during the war. By 1949 Stanford had become one of the top three recipients of government research contracts, overshadowing all other electronics departments west of the Mississippi River.

In 1951 Terman spearheaded the creation of the Stanford Industrial (now Research) Park, which granted long-term leases on university land exclusively to high-technology firms. Soon Varian Associates, Inc. (now Varian Medical

XEROX PARC

The Xerox Corporation Palo Alto Research Center (PARC) was established in 1970 by Xerox Corp. to explore new information technologies that were not necessarily related to the paper copier market, which Xerox had invented in 1948 and dominated ever since. Upon opening the facility in Palo Alto, George Pake, the director of the new centre, went about assembling a staff. His first hire was Robert Taylor, a former deputy director of the Advanced Research Projects Agency (ARPA), which had established a government-sponsored network of research databases that played a key role in creating the Internet. At ARPA Taylor had been at the centre of a network of people engaged in advanced research. Choosing from his vast array of contacts, he was able to staff PARC with the visionary researchers that Pake wanted. Commercial products might not appear for a decade, but prize-winning ideas would develop quickly, and Xerox would be the first to profit.

Or such was the plan. As events transpired, the 1970s were a decade of fundamental innovation at PARC, but its parent company failed to transform these ideas into dollars. Among the many inventions, few were as important as the Xerox Alto, the first personal computer, developed in 1973. By the time its commercial version, the Xerox Star, was released in 1981, at a price of more than $16,000 per machine, new computer companies such as Apple Computer, Inc. already had released more affordable machines; even the giant International Business Machines Corp. (IBM) had released a relatively inexpensive personal computer, the IBM PC. The Star, however, with its mouse-driven graphical user interface, built-in Ethernet networking protocol, and optional laser printer, was far ahead of its time. It remained for other companies to cash in on Xerox's innovations.

The story of the laser printer, a technology developed by Gary Starkweather, a researcher at Xerox, epitomizes the company's inability to capitalize quickly on innovation. Starkweather realized that short exposures, on the order of a billionth of a second from a laser, could replace the Xerox photocopier's traditional light source. More important, a laser-driven copier could also serve as a printer, taking an image from a computer screen and capturing it on paper. No longer would computer printers be restricted to producing text. Instead, anything displayable on a computer monitor could be printed. The idea of "what you see is what you get"—WYSIWYG—would work on paper as well as the monitor. Unfortunately, at that time Xerox saw no point in innovating when their current technology worked so well. Only intervention by Jack Goldman, the director of research at Xerox, saved the idea when he had Starkweather transferred to PARC in 1971. By early 1972 a working prototype existed, though Xerox did not bring it to market until 1977. The laser printer soon became a best-selling product.

Another early PARC breakthrough was the Ethernet. Proposed by Robert Metcalfe and jointly developed with Intel Corporation and Digital Equipment Corporation in the mid-1970s, this networking standard increased the speed and reliability of data exchanges over local area networks (LANs). The Ethernet is still commonly used in small offices and in homes to link computers and printers.

Systems, Inc.), Eastman Kodak Co., General Electric Co., Admiral Corp., Lockheed Corp. (now Lockheed Martin Corp.), Hewlett-Packard, and others turned Stanford Research Park into America's premier high-technology manufacturing region. A mutually beneficial relationship developed wherein professors consulted with the rent-paying tenants, industrial researchers taught courses on campus, and companies recruited the best students. The park was Silicon Valley in miniature. As more firms moved to the region, fueling demand for basic electronic components, technical skills, and business supplies, many former high-technology employees started their own companies. Long before the personal computer, the "start-up" was the culture of the Valley.

FROM SEMICONDUCTORS TO PERSONAL COMPUTERS

In 1956 William Shockley, Nobel Prize–winning coinventor of the transistor, established his new Shockley Semiconductor Laboratory in the park. Within a year a group of dissatisfied engineers resigned en masse to join with Fairchild Camera and Instrument Corporation to establish Fairchild Semiconductor Corporation in nearby Santa Clara. (Engineers from Fairchild went on to coinvent the integrated circuit in 1958.) This was the first of many corporate fractures that shaped the American semiconductor landscape. Of 31 semiconductor manufacturers established in the United States during the 1960s, only five existed outside the Valley; the remainder were the result of different engineers leaving Fairchild.

The late 1960s and early 1970s saw a fundamental change in the semiconductor market. By 1972 the U.S. military accounted for only 12 percent of semiconductor sales, compared with more than 50 percent during the early 1960s. Consumer applications grew until, by the mid-1970s, venture capitalists had replaced the U.S. government as the primary source of financing for start-ups. Meanwhile, entrepreneurs were quickly establishing firms to supply the semiconductor manufacturers with everything from instruments and measurement equipment to furnaces and cubicle partitions. In Silicon Valley it was possible to establish a corporation, find venture capital, rent space, hire staff, and be in business within a matter of weeks.

In the 1980s and '90s the Silicon Valley landscape changed further as the economy shifted from semiconductors to personal computer manufacturing, and then to computer software and Internet-based business. Economic growth during the transitional period 1986–92 was an anemic 0.7 percent per year, leading many manufacturers in the region to demand government protection from foreign competitors. Nevertheless, Stanford students continued to establish roughly 100 new companies each year, including Sun Microsystems, Inc. in 1982 and Yahoo! Inc. in 1994. Successful entrepreneurs returned as venture capitalists to plow their expertise and wealth back into the Valley. The intellectual density of the Valley grew, and the constant movement of employees and skills continued.

Yet, through all this frenetic growth, personal contact remained central to the Valley way of doing business. Indeed, personal relationships were as important in the age of the Internet as they were when the U.S. government gave out military research funding in the early years of the Valley's development. A venture capitalist might read thousands of business plans, but it was usually the personal presentation and the personality of the entrepreneur that determined funding. A poor presentation would sink all but the most brilliant plan. This was one of the great ironies of the boom economy of the 1990s. While the Internet enabled global communications, many of the technologies that made this transformation possible were the product of a local culture of face-to-face interaction.

From Boom to Bust to Boom

Since the invention of the integrated circuit, Silicon Valley and growth have been nearly synonymous. In 1959 there were roughly 18,000 high-technology jobs in the area. By 1971 there were approximately 117,000 such jobs, and in 1990 nearly 268,000 filled positions. From 1992 to 1999, Silicon Valley added more than 230,000 jobs (an increase of 23 percent) and accounted for roughly 40 percent of California's export trade. To fill the growing need for high-technology workers, particularly engineers, the United States relaxed immigration quotas for aliens with special training, and the region experienced a large influx of workers from India and China. From 1975 to the 1990 U.S. census, the foreign-born population of Santa Clara county more than doubled, to 350,000. By the 21st century the

Valley's population had grown to more than two million. San Jose alone grew from roughly 200,000 in 1960 to more than 900,000 by century's end to become the largest city in northern California. Electronics, computers, and computer software made the region's wealth, but much of that wealth was absorbed by real estate; by 2000 the median price of a home in Santa Clara county was more than twice the national median for major metropolitan areas.

The year 2000 marked the end of the "Internet bubble," a five-year period when the paper value of publicly traded stock in Internet-based companies rose far above the real earning potential of the industry. By 2005 publicly traded Valley firms were worth roughly one-third of their market peak—a paper loss of approximately $2 trillion. Economic change of that magnitude had a profound effect. In 2005 there were fewer jobs in Santa Clara county than before the boom began in 1995. Venture capital funding, the lifeblood of Valley start-ups, collapsed from $105.5 billion in 2000 to $20.9 billion in 2004. When the separate housing bubble burst in 2008, along with the general economy, the median sale price of homes in the Valley tumbled more than 30 percent during the year, with some areas experiencing a nearly 50 percent drop in housing prices.

Yet even though Silicon Valley's famous optimism took a beating in the post-bubble environment, it was not knocked out. In the aftermath of the Great Recession of 2008–09, with unemployment rates in the Valley at 10 percent or more, newcomers such as LinkedIn and Facebook raised hopes that social media might be the next new wave to keep the Valley's fortunes afloat. Even in a period of reduced investment, Silicon Valley companies drew as much as 40 percent of all venture capital funding in the United States.

Such statistics are important but they cannot capture the essence of the Valley or the history that has made such a remarkable place possible. Most current residents see the Valley as a product of raw, naked capitalism, a place where cubicle workers exist on a diet of fast food, venture capitalists drive luxury cars and specialize in particular types of computer chips, and bright young men and women can pitch their ideas, obtain financial support, and wait for the initial public offering of stock in their enterprise to transform them from hardworking individuals into hardworking millionaires. Of course, after the bursting of the Internet bubble and the general recession almost a decade later, residents realized that expectations of constant, unimpeded growth were not simply foolish but dangerous. Historical amnesia is an important part of Valley culture, but even its emphasis on the "new new thing" cannot erase the fact that the region's economic power is a product of its past as well as its present, of military contracts as well as venture capital. Silicon Valley is an economically mature region whose childhood and adolescence were paid for by U.S. tax dollars.

FROM THE COLD WAR TO THE COUNTERCULTURE

The Internet has evolved from the integration of two very different technological agendas—the Cold War networking of the U.S. military and the personal computer (PC) revolution. The first agenda can be dated to 1973, when the Defense Advanced Research Projects Agency (DARPA) sought to create a communications network that would support the transfer of large data files between government and government-sponsored academic-research laboratories. The result was the ARPANET, a robust decentralized network that supported a vast array of computer hardware. Initially, ARPANET was the preserve of academics and corporate researchers with access

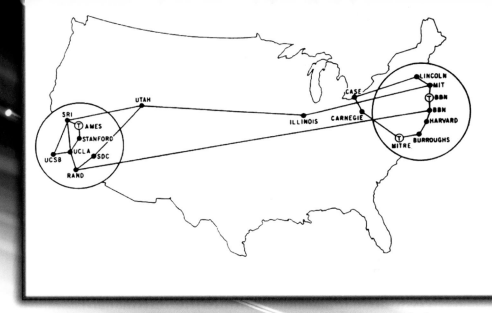

A 1972 map detailing the communication centres and relays of the ARPANET—the precursor of today's Internet. Apic/Hulton Archive/ Getty Images

to time-sharing mainframe computer systems. Computers were large and expensive; most computer professionals could not imagine anyone needing, let alone owning, his own "personal" computer. Yet Joseph Licklider, one of the driving forces at DARPA for computer networking, stated that online communication would "change the nature and value of communication even more profoundly than did the printing press and the picture tube."

The second agenda began to emerge in 1977 with the introduction of the Apple II, the first affordable computer for individuals and small businesses. Created by Apple Computer, Inc. (now Apple Inc.), the Apple II was popular in schools by 1979, but in the corporate market it was stigmatized as a game machine. The task of cracking the business market fell to IBM. In 1981 the IBM PC was released, immediately standardizing the PC's basic hardware and operating system—so much so that first "PC-compatible" and then simply "PC" came to mean any personal computer built along the lines of the IBM PC.

A major centre of the PC revolution was the San Francisco Bay area, where several major research institutions funded by DARPA—Stanford University, the University of California, Berkeley, and Xerox PARC—provided much of the technical foundation for Silicon Valley. It was no small coincidence that Apple's two young founders, Steven Jobs and Stephen Wozniak, worked as interns in the Stanford University Artificial Intelligence Laboratory and at nearby Hewlett-Packard. The Bay Area's counterculture also figured prominently in the PC's history. Electronic hobbyists saw themselves in open revolt against the "priesthood" of the mainframe computer and worked together in computer-enthusiast groups to spread computing to the masses.

The military played an essential role in shaping the Internet's architecture, but it was through the counterculture that many of the practices of contemporary online life emerged. A telling example is the early electronic bulletin board system (BBS), such as the WELL (Whole Earth 'Lectronic Link). Established in 1985 by American publisher Stewart Brand, who viewed the BBS as an extension of his *Whole Earth Catalog*, the WELL was one of the first electronic communities organized around forums dedicated to particular subjects such as parenting and Grateful Dead concerts. The latter were an especially popular topic of online conversation, but it was in the parenting forum where a profound sense of community and belonging initially appeared. For example, when one participant's child was diagnosed with leukemia, members of the forum went out of their way either to find health resources or to comfort the distressed parents.

In this one instance, several features still prevalent in the online world can be seen. Foremost among them is the fact that geography was irrelevant. WELL members in California and New York could bring their knowledge together within the confines of a forum—and could do so collectively, often exceeding the experience available to any local physician or medical centre. This marshaling of shared resources persists to this day as many individuals use the Internet to learn more about their ailments, find others who suffer from the same disease, and learn about drugs, physicians, and alternative therapies.

E-mail, Smart Mobs, and Social Consciousness

For the individual, the Internet opened up new communication possibilities. E-mail, which quickly led to a substantial decline in traditional "snail mail," was soon followed by instant messaging (IM), or short message service (SMS) text messaging—especially among youth--which flourished given the convergence of the Internet and cellular telephones. Indeed, texting has become a particular problem in classrooms, where students often surreptitiously exchange notes, and on the road, where texting has received increasing blame for causing traffic accidents. The average American cell phone is now used far more often to send a text message than it is to place a voice call.

From mailing lists to "buddy lists," e-mail and SMS have been used to create "smart mobs" that converge in the physical world for common action. Examples include protest organizing, spontaneous performance art, and shopping. Obviously, people congregated before the Internet existed; the change wrought by mass e-mailing and SMS has been in the speed of assembling such events. For example, in February 1999, activists began planning protests against the November 1999 World Trade Organization (WTO) meetings in Seattle, Washington. Using the Internet, organizers mobilized more than 50,000 individuals from around the world to engage in demonstrations—at times violent—that effectively altered the WTO's agenda. More than a decade later, in June 2010, Egyptian computer engineer Wael Ghonim anonymously created a page titled "We Are All Khaled Said" on the social media site Facebook to publicize the death of a 28-year-old Egyptian man beaten to death by police. The page garnered hundreds of thousands of members, becoming an online forum for the discussion of police brutality in Egypt. After a popular uprising in Tunisia in January 2011, Ghonim and several other Internet democracy activists posted messages to their sites calling for similar action in Egypt. Their social media campaign helped spur mass demonstrations that forced Egyptian Pres. Hosni Mubarak from power.

The convergence of mobs is not without some techno-silliness. "Flash mobs"—groups of strangers who are mobilized on short notice via Web sites, online discussion groups, or e-mail distribution lists—often take part in bizarre though usually harmless activities in public places, such as engaging in mass free-for-alls around the world on Pillow Fight Day. While flash-mob antics tend to be silly, some experts conjecture that they hold the promise of organizing people for more practical purposes, such as political demonstrations.

In the wake of catastrophic disasters, citizens have used the Internet to donate to charities in an unprecedented fashion. Others have used the Internet to reunite family members or to match lost pets with their owners. The role of the Internet in responding to disasters, both natural and deliberate, remains the topic of much discussion, as it is unclear whether the Internet actually can function in a

Members of a group called the Clean Air Network stage a flash mob protest against poor air quality in the streets of Hong Kong on June 5, 2011. Ed Jones/ AFP/Getty Images

disaster area when much of the infrastructure is destroyed. Certainly during the attacks of September 11, 2001, people found it easier to communicate with loved ones in New York City via e-mail than through the overwhelmed telephone network. Following the earthquake that struck Haiti in January 2010, electronic media emerged as a useful mode for connecting those separated by the quake and for coordinating relief efforts. Survivors who were able to access the Internet—and friends and relatives abroad—took to social networking sites such as Facebook in search of information on those missing in the wake of the catastrophe. Feeds from these sites also assisted aid organizations in constructing maps of the areas affected and determining where to channel resources. The many

Haitians lacking Internet access were able to contribute updates via text messaging on mobile phones.

Social Gaming and Social Networking

One-to-one or even one-to-many communication is only the most elementary form of Internet social life. The very nature of the Internet makes spatial distances largely irrelevant for social interactions. Online gaming has moved from simply playing a game with friends to a rather complex form of social life in which the game's virtual reality spills over into the physical world. The case of *World of Warcraft*, a popular electronic game with several million players, is one example. Property acquired in the game can be sold online, although such secondary economies are discouraged by Blizzard, the publisher of *World of Warcraft*, as a violation of the game's terms of service. In any case, what does it mean that one can own virtual property and that someone is willing to pay for this property with real money? Economists have begun studying such virtual economies, some of which now exceed the gross national product of countries in Africa and Asia. In fact, virtual economies finally have given economists a means of running controlled experiments.

Millions of people have created online game characters for entertainment purposes. Gaming creates an online community, but it also allows for a blurring of the boundaries between the real world and the virtual one. In Shanghai one gamer stabbed and killed another one in the real world over a virtual sword used in *Legend of Mir 3*. Although attempts were made to involve the authorities in the original dispute, the police found themselves at a loss prior to the murder because the law did not acknowledge the existence of virtual property. In South Korea violence surrounding online gaming happens often enough that police refer to such murders as "off-line PK," a reference to player killing (PK), or player-versus-player lethal contests, which are allowed or encouraged in some games. South Korean police have been forced to create special cybercrime units to patrol both within the game and offline. Potential problems from such games are not limited to crime. Virtual life can be addictive. Reports of players neglecting family, school, work, and even their health to the point of death have become common.

Social networking sites (SNSs) have emerged as a significant online phenomenon since the bursting of the Internet "bubble" in the early 2000s. SNSs use software to facilitate online communities, where members with shared interests swap files, photographs, videos, and music, send messages and chat, set up blogs (Web diaries) and discussion groups, and share opinions. Early social networking services included Classmates.com, which connected former schoolmates, and Yahoo! 360° and SixDegrees, which built networks of connections via friends of friends. In the post-"bubble" era the leading social networking services were MySpace, Facebook, Friendster, Orkut, and LinkedIn. LinkedIn became an effective tool for business staff recruiting. Businesses have begun to exploit these networks, drawing on social networking research and theory which suggests that finding key "influential" members of existing networks of individuals can give access to and credibility with the whole network.

CHAPTER 2

AN OPEN WORLD

G iven its roots in the counterculture of the late 20th century, it is no surprise that the Internet has brought with it new ideas of how to reorganize not only information, but all of society. Among many Internet-using citizens, social networks are no longer considered to be tied to physical location, transparency and openness are seen as the surest means to material and social progress, and hierarchy is to be abandoned in favour of the self-correcting power of communities.

VIRTUAL COMMUNITIES

A virtual community is a group of people, who may or may not meet one another face-to-face, who exchange words and ideas through the mediation of computer bulletin board systems (BBSs) and other digital networks.

The first use of the phrase *virtual community* appeared in a 1987 article written by Howard Rheingold for *The Whole Earth Review*. In *The Virtual Community* (1993), Rheingold expanded on his article to offer the following definition:

> *Virtual communities are social aggregations that emerge from the Net when enough people carry on those public discussions long enough, with sufficient human feeling, to form webs of personal relationships in cyberspace.*

Rheingold's article and book are cited as the foundational works of cyberculture studies. Many subsequent

Douglas Engelbart of the Stanford Research Institute. In addition to his pioneering work with online virtual communities, Engelbart is credited with inventing the computer mouse. Apic/Hulton Archive/Getty Images

commentators have contested his use of the word *community* and the terminology used to describe the technosocial phenomena of persistent computer-mediated relationships; *social media* and *participatory media* are also used to describe a very broad variety of human social activity online.

The first predictions of communities of computer-linked individuals and groups were made in 1968 by J.C.R. Licklider and Robert Taylor, who as research administrators for the U.S. Defense Advanced Research Projects Agency (DARPA) set in motion the research that resulted in the creation of the first such community, the ARPANET, which was the precursor of the Internet. Licklider and Taylor wrote,

> *What will on-line interactive communities be like? In most fields they will consist of geographically separated members, sometimes grouped in small clusters and sometimes working individually. They will be communities not of common location, but of common interest.*

Even before the ARPANET, in the early 1960s, the PLATO computer-based education system included online community features. Douglas Engelbart, who ran the ARPANET's first Network Information Center, had grown a "bootstrapping community" at the Stanford Research Institute (SRI), located at Stanford University in California, through use of his pioneering oNLine System (NLS) before the ARPANET was launched.

By the beginning of the 21st century, the four computer nodes (University of California at Los Angeles, SRI, University of California at Santa Barbara, and University of Utah) that constituted the ARPANET community in 1969 had expanded to include some one billion people with access to the Internet. With several billion mobile telephones now in existence and the proliferation of Internet connections in mobile devices, it is likely that a significant portion of the human population conducts some of their social affairs by means of computer networks. The range of networked activities has greatly expanded since Rheingold described BBSs, chat rooms, mailing lists, USENET newsgroups, and MUDs (multiuser dungeons) in 1993. In the 21st century, people meet, play, conduct discourse, socialize, do business, and organize collective action through instant messages, blogs (including videoblogs), RSS feeds (a format for subscribing to and receiving regularly updated content from Web sites), wikis, social network services, photo and media-sharing communities such as Flickr, massively multiplayer online games such as *Lineage* and *World of Warcraft*, and immersive virtual worlds such as Second Life. Some services, such as Twitter and Facebook, combine features of some or all of these media. Virtual communities and social media have coevolved as emerging technologies have afforded new kinds of interaction and as different groups of people have appropriated media for new purposes.

The emergence of a globally networked public has raised a number of psychological, sociological, economic, and political issues, and these issues, in turn, have stimulated the creation of new courses and research programs in social media, virtual communities, and cyberculture studies. In particular, the widespread use of online communication tools has raised questions of identity and the presentation of self, community or pseudocommunity, collective action, public sphere, social capital, and quality of attention.

A number of different critiques arose as cyberculture studies emerged. A political critique of early online activism questioned whether online relationships offered a

USENET

USENET, or "User's Network," an Internet-based network of discussion groups, began in 1979 when two graduate students at Duke University in Durham, N.C., Tom Truscott and Jim Ellis, came up with a way to exchange messages and files between computers using UNIX-to-UNIX copy protocol (UUCP). Steve Bellovin, a graduate student at the University of North Carolina (UNC) at Chapel Hill, wrote the software that controlled this first version of the network. USENET officially began in 1980 in North Carolina with three networked computers, located at UNC, Duke, and Duke Medical School. Many improvements were developed over the years, including the creation of the more efficient network news transfer protocol (NNTP).

Over time, USENET grew to include thousands of discussion groups (called newsgroups), stored on special Internet servers, and millions of users. Users read and write posts, called articles, using software called a newsreader. (Modern Web browsers and e-mail software typically contain a built-in newsreader, eliminating the need for a separate program.) Each newsgroup covers a specific topic, and most new newsgroups have to go through an approval process. Alternative newsgroups, however, can be created by anyone and can cover nearly any subject. Newsgroups can be either moderated (every article is pre-approved) or unmoderated.

Unmoderated and alternative newsgroups have led to controversy. The lack of oversight and the anonymity of USENET has attracted people who post pornography and other indecent material. In addition, USENET has facilitated the illegal sharing of copyrighted material, such as software, music, and movies. This has led to anti-piracy measures enacted by governments and private companies. Despite the adoption of peer-to-peer (P2P) software, pirates often prefer the anonymous nature of the network. Yet USENET remains popular with a wide variety of legitimate users as well. The American search engine company Google Inc. has added more than 20 years of USENET archives to its service Google Groups.

kind of comforting simulation of collective action. On close inspection, the question of what actually defines a community has turned out to be complex: American sociologist George A. Hillery, Jr., compiled 92 different definitions. Canadian sociologist Barry Wellman defined community as "networks of interpersonal ties that provide sociability, support, information, a sense of belonging, and social identity"—and offered empirical evidence that at least some virtual communities fit these criteria. As has happened in the past, what people mean when they speak of community is shifting.

As the early digital enthusiasts, builders, and researchers were joined by a more representative sample of the world's population, a broader and not always wholesome representation of human behaviour manifested itself online. Life online in the 21st century enabled terrorists and various cybercriminals to make use of the same many-to-many digital networks that enable support groups for disease victims and caregivers, disaster relief action, distance learning, and community-building efforts. Soldiers in battle taunt their enemies with text messages, disseminate information through instant messaging, and communicate home through online videos. With so many young people spending so much of their time online, many parents and "real world" community leaders expressed concerns about the possible effects of overindulging in such virtual social lives. In addition, in an environment where anyone can publish anything or make any claim online, the need to include an understanding of social media in education has given rise to advocates for "participatory pedagogy."

Students of online social behaviour have noted a shift from "group-centric" characterizations of online socializing to a perspective that takes into account "networked individualism." Again, quoting Wellman:

Although people often view the world in terms of groups, they function in networks. In networked societies: boundaries are permeable, interactions are with diverse others, connections switch between multiple networks, and hierarchies can be flatter and recursive....Most people operate in multiple, thinly-connected, partial communities as they deal with networks of kin, neighbours, friends, workmates and organizational ties. Rather than fitting into the same group as those around them, each person has his/her own "personal community."

It is likely that community-centred forms of online communication will continue to flourish; in the medical community alone, mutual support groups will continue to afford strong and persistent bonds between people whose primary communications take place online. At the same time, it is also likely that the prevalence of individual-centred social network services and the proliferation of personal communication devices will feed the evolution of "networked individualism." Cyberculture studies, necessarily an interdisciplinary pursuit, is likely to continue to grow as more human socialization is mediated by digital networks.

THE OPEN-SOURCE MOVEMENT

"Open source," in the social sense, is the name of a movement begun by computer programmers that rejects secrecy and centralized control of creative work in favour of decentralization, transparency, and unrestricted ("open") sharing of information. "Source" refers to the human-readable source code of computer programs, as opposed to the compiled computer programming language instructions, or object code, that run on computers but cannot be easily understood or modified by people.

In closed-source, or proprietary, software development, only the object code is published; the source code is held secret in order to control customers and markets. Open-source projects reject this practice and publish all their source code on the Internet under licenses that allow free redistribution. An important feature of open-source development is that the resulting extensive peer review seems to do a better job of minimizing computer bugs and computer security risks than the typical in-house process of quality assurance at closed-source vendors.

Beyond computer software, the concept of open source has been used to create free online databases and by commercial Internet vendors to populate reviews of items for sale, such as books, music, and movies.

ROOTS IN HACKER CULTURE

The roots of open source go back to computer science practices in the 1960s in academia and early computer user groups. Computer programmers frequently and informally shared code that they had written ("hacked"), quickly recycling and freely modifying code that solved common technical problems. Several different technical cultures began to develop, in parallel and semi-independently, practices similar to modern open-source development, although without today's apparatus of common licenses and fast communication via the Internet.

The practice of sharing code was most effective and consistent among developers of the UNIX operating system, which was central to UNIX's early success. UNIX was first developed about 1970 at the Bell Laboratories subsidiary of the AT&T Corporation for use on the Digital Equipment Corporation PDP-7 minicomputer. As UNIX was adapted for various computer hardware systems, new variants of the operating system were developed. By the time that AT&T and Sun Microsystems, Inc. (a proponent of the UNIX variant developed at the University of California, Berkeley), finally decided to commercialize UNIX in 1987, a large segment of computer manufacturers and software developers decided that they needed an "open" system and formed the Open Software Foundation. This set off the so-called "UNIX wars" among minicomputer enthusiasts.

The shift from informal sharing of code to explicit open-source practice actually began a few years earlier with Richard M. Stallman, a charismatic programmer who had thrived in the computer science environment at the Massachusetts Institute of Technology (MIT) but collided with the increasing commercialization of software in the early 1980s. With more companies blocking access to their source codes, Stallman felt frustrated in his efforts to fix and improve these codes, so he decided that proprietary software must be publicly opposed. In 1984 he

Richard M. Stallman lectures at St. Joseph's College in Bangalore, India, in 2006. Stallman is a founding member of the Free Software Movement.

resigned from MIT to found the GNU Project, with the goal of developing a completely free UNIX-like operating system. (GNU is a recursive acronym for "GNU's not UNIX.") In 1985 he delivered the "GNU Manifesto" outlining his program of free software development, formed the Free Software Foundation (FSF), and launched what he called the free software movement.

Stallman may have been the first to propose a label for what many computer programmers had been doing all along, but the term *free software* was never universally accepted among programmers. Before Stallman issued the "GNU Manifesto," few programmers had any sense of being members of a social movement, and, once that sense developed, Stallman's label carried too much ideological freight for many of them.

In pursuit of his ends, Stallman wrote the General Public License (GPL), a document attached to computer code that would legally require anyone distributing that code to make available any of their modifications and distributed works (a property Stallman called "copyleft"). In effect, he sought to codify the hacker ethos. By the end of the century, the GPL was the license of choice for approximately half of all open-source projects. The other half was divided among non-copyleft licenses, notably the MIT license, and various licenses based on the Berkeley Software Distribution (BSD), developed in the 1970s at the University of California at Berkeley.

After 1987 the availability of Intel Corporation's 32-bit 386 microprocessor meant that inexpensive personal computers (PCs) had sufficient power to run UNIX—in fact, the SCO Group released the first version of UNIX to run on the 386 that year. Some programmers who had been key players in the development of the BSD variant of UNIX founded a project called 386BSD to port that variant to PCs. The Free Software Foundation's HURD operating system project also refocused on the 386-based PC. But both projects lagged at a critical time, 386BSD because of a lawsuit and HURD because of unrealistic design goals.

THE LINUX PLATFORM

By 1991 Internet access had become sufficiently common that e-mail could knit together a large, worldwide community of volunteer developers and function as an effective distribution medium for software. The FSF and the 386BSD project were slow to grasp these possibilities. Linus Torvalds, a student at Finland's University of Helsinki, stepped into the gap. Using the GPL and programming tools from the GNU Project, in 1991 he announced an Internet-centred effort to develop a PC UNIX of his own—Linux.

Linux was the first major Internet-centred open-source project. Torvalds encouraged contributions from everyone and issued updated releases of the kernel (the UNIX-like operating system at the core of Linux) at an unprecedented pace—weekly, sometimes even daily. The developer community around Linux grew with astonishing speed, absorbing refugees from the stagnation of the HURD project and the legal uncertainties surrounding BSD. By 1995 what would later be called the open-source community had become aware of itself as a community, and it increasingly adopted Linux as a common platform.

Although Linux was not as user-friendly as the popular Microsoft Windows and Mac OS operating systems, it was an efficient and reliable system that rarely crashed. Combined with Apache, an open-source Web server, Linux accounted for more than a third of all servers used on the Internet. Because it was open source, and thus modifiable for different uses, Linux was popular for systems as diverse as cellular telephones and supercomputers.

Oracle Corp. CEO Larry Ellison speaks in front of a screen touting the company's latest Linux program in 2006. One of Linux's claims to fame is that it rarely crashes. Justin Sullivan/Getty Images

The addition of user-friendly desktop environments, office suites, Web browsers, and even games helped to increase Linux's popularity and make it more suitable for home and office desktops. New distributions (packages of Linux software) were created throughout the 1990s. Some of the more well-known distributions included Red Hat, Debian, and Slackware.

"THE CATHEDRAL & THE BAZAAR"

In 1997 computer programmer Eric Raymond proposed a new theory of open source in his paper "The Cathedral & the Bazaar." Raymond compared the centralization, secrecy, slow-release tempo, and vertical management of traditional software development to a cathedral with its top-down hierarchal structure. The decentralization, transparency, openness, and peer networking of the Linux community he likened to a bazaar, with its give-and-take negotiations. The paper advanced reasons that the bazaar-like distributed approach to software development could be expected to yield higher-quality software.

Where Stallman had framed his argument primarily in moral terms ("information needs to be free"), Raymond spoke in terms of engineering, rational choice, and market economics. He summed up his argument with this maxim: "Given a sufficiently large number of eyeballs, all [computer] bugs are shallow." In early 1998 Raymond proposed the term *open source* as a description of the same community practices that Stallman had previously promoted under the *free software* phrase. With Raymond's proposal—and replacement of the label *free*—came a new program of outreach to corporations and the media.

Under the open-source banner, the movement made huge strides during the "dot-com boom" of 1998–2000, and it kept those gains in the stock market bust that followed. By 2003 early doubts about whether open source could be the basis for a viable business model had been largely resolved. The open-source community's commercial partners included both midsized firms with community roots (such as Red Hat Software, Inc.) and large corporations (such as IBM and the Hewlett-Packard Company) intent on capturing the efficiencies and marketing pull of open source.

In the new climate, governments in the United States and around the world began to question the wisdom of relying on proprietary code, which they could neither examine nor modify. Open-source advocates argued, with some success, that reliance on proprietary software could leave governments open to dangerous security breaches that software providers might be slow to fix. In contrast, they argued that the independent scrutiny of open-source programs offered the most effective possible audit. More political pressure developed when governments outside the United States began to wonder why they were paying large licensing fees to foreign corporations, especially when open source would make it possible to localize software for language communities too small for those foreign corporations to invest in serving.

In Raymond's view, the shift to open source is being forced by the failure of other software verification methods to scale up as software becomes more complex—a view that has moved from mere speculation to nearly conventional wisdom within the open-source community. There remains, however, some political tension in the community between free software purists and pragmatists, with the former sometimes insisting on an identity separate from the rest of the open-source movement. This fissure roughly parallels the split between GPL and non-copyleft licences such as BSD and MIT.

Technically, the open-source community remains close to its UNIX roots. The largest and most important faction remains the development network around the Linux operating system, which is fast eclipsing older UNIX variants. Other prestigious and significant open-source projects include the Apache World Wide Web server, the Firefox Web browser, the Perl and Python computer languages, and Stallman's Emacs editor.

While Stallman, Torvalds, and Raymond have been relatively reluctant to discuss the application of open-source principles outside of software, others have been inspired by them. *Wikipedia*, a free, user-edited online encyclopaedia, was founded in explicit imitation of the open-source programming movement, as was the open publications movement in the sciences and the open genomics movement in bioinformatics. The influence of open-source

A screenshot showing the Mozilla Firefox logo as the company prepared to celebrate the billionth download of its free Web browser in 2009. Leon Neal/ AFP/Getty Images

programming philosophy (and the code it has built) is pervasive in Web-based social networking sites such as eBay, Amazon, LiveJournal, and MySpace, where comments and product reviews are an essential feature of their commercial success and popularity. Perhaps most significant for future economic development around the world, visionaries are seeking ways to harness the "many-eyeballs effect" with networked organizations that emulate the observed structure of open-source software development teams.

WIKIPEDIA AND COLLABORATIVE INFORMATION

Wikipedia is a free Internet-based encyclopaedia, started in 2001, that operates under an open-source management style. It is overseen by the nonprofit Wikimedia Foundation. *Wikipedia* uses a collaborative software known as wiki that facilitates the creation and development of articles. Although some highly publicized problems have called attention to *Wikipedia*'s editorial process, they have done little to dampen public use of the resource, which is one of the most-visited sites on the Internet.

Origin and Growth

In 1996 Jimmy Wales, a successful bond trader, moved to San Diego, Calif., to establish Bomis, Inc., a Web portal company. In March 2000 Wales founded *Nupedia*, a free online encyclopaedia, with Larry Sanger as editor-in-chief. *Nupedia* was organized like existing encyclopaedias, with an advisory board of experts and a lengthy review process. By January 2001 fewer than two dozen articles were finished, and Sanger advocated supplementing *Nupedia* with an open-source encyclopaedia. On Jan. 15, 2001, *Wikipedia* was launched as a feature of Nupedia.com, but, following objections from the advisory board, it was relaunched as an independent Web site a few days later. In its first year *Wikipedia* expanded to some 20,000 articles in 18 languages, including French, German, Polish, Dutch, Hebrew, Chinese, and Esperanto. In 2003 *Nupedia* was terminated and its articles moved into *Wikipedia*.

By 2006 the English-language version of *Wikipedia* had more than one million articles, and by the time of its 10th anniversary in 2011 it had surpassed 3.5 million. However, while the encyclopaedia continued to expand at a rate of millions of words per month, the number of new articles created each year gradually decreased, from a peak of 665,000 in 2007 to 374,000 in 2010. In response to this slowdown, the Wikimedia Foundation began to focus its expansion efforts on the non-English versions of *Wikipedia*, which by early 2011 numbered more than 250. With some versions having already amassed hundreds of thousands of articles—the French and German versions both boasted more than one million—particular attention was paid to languages of the developing world, such as Swahili and Tamil, in an attempt to reach populations otherwise underserved by the Internet. One impediment to *Wikipedia*'s ability to reach a truly global audience, however, was the Chinese government's periodic restrictions of access to some or all of the site's content within China.

Principles and Procedures

In some respects *Wikipedia*'s open-source production model is the epitome of the so-called Web 2.0, an egalitarian environment where the web of social software enmeshes users in both their real and virtual-reality workplaces. The *Wikipedia* community is based on a limited number of standard principles. One important principle is neutrality. Another is the faith that contributors are

Wikipedia founder Jimmy Wales speaks at a computing conference in 2006.
Mario Tama/Getty Images

participating in a sincere and deliberate fashion. Readers can correct what they perceive to be errors, and disputes over facts and over possible bias are conducted through contributor discussions. Three other guiding principles are to keep within the defined parameters of an encyclopaedia, to respect copyright laws, and to consider any other rules to be flexible. The last principle reinforces the project's belief that the open-source process will make *Wikipedia* into the best product available, given its community of users. At the very least, one by-product of the process is that the encyclopaedia contains a number of publicly accessible pages that are not necessarily classifiable as articles. These include stubs, which are very short articles intended to be expanded, and talk pages, which contain discussions between contributors.

The central policy of inviting readers to serve as authors or editors creates the potential for problems as well as their at least partial solution. Not all users are scrupulous about providing accurate information, and *Wikipedia* must also deal with individuals who deliberately deface particular articles, post misleading or false statements, or add obscene material. *Wikipedia*'s method is to rely on its users to monitor and clean up its articles. Trusted contributors can also receive administrator privileges that provide access to an array of software tools to speedily fix Web graffiti and other serious problems.

ISSUES AND CONTROVERSIES

Reliance on community self-policing has generated some problems. In 2005 the American journalist John Seigenthaler, Sr., discovered that his *Wikipedia* biography falsely identified him as a potential conspirator in the assassinations of both John F. Kennedy and Robert

F. Kennedy and that these malicious claims had survived *Wikipedia*'s community policing for 132 days. The author of this information could not be easily identified, since all that is known about unregistered contributors is their computers' IP, or Internet protocol, addresses, many of which are dynamically generated each time a user goes online. (The contributor later confessed and apologized, saying that he wrote the false information as a joke.)

The Seigenthaler case prompted *Wikipedia* to prohibit unregistered users from editing certain articles. Similar instances of vandalism later led site administrators to formulate a procedure, despite protests from some contributors, by which some edits would be reviewed by experienced editors before the changes could appear online.

Although *Wikipedia* has occasionally come under fire for including information not intended to be widely disseminated—such as images of the 10 inkblots used by psychologists in the Rorschach Test—it has also adapted its philosophy of openness in certain cases. For instance, after *New York Times* reporter David S. Rohde was kidnapped by Taliban militants in Afghanistan in 2008, his employer arranged with *Wikipedia* for news of the incident to be kept off the Web site on the grounds that it could endanger Rohde's life. The site's administrators complied, in the face of repeated attempts by users to add the information, until after Rohde's eventual escape. Additionally, in 2010 it was revealed that there was a cache of pornographic images, including illegal depictions of sexual acts involving children, on Wikimedia Commons, a site maintained by the Wikimedia Foundation that served as a repository of media files for use in all Wikimedia products. Although there were no such illegal images on *Wikipedia* itself, the ensuing scandal prompted Jimmy Wales, who personally deleted many of the Commons files, to encourage administrators to remove any prurient content from Wikimedia sites.

Wikipedia administrators also have the power to block particular IP addresses—a power they used in 2006 after it was found that staff members of some U.S. congressional representatives had altered articles to eliminate unfavourable details. News of such self-interested editing inspired Virgil Griffith, a graduate student at the California Institute of Technology, to create Wikipedia Scanner, or WikiScanner, in 2007. By correlating the IP addresses attached to every *Wikipedia* edit with their owners, Griffith constructed a database that he made available on the Web for anyone to search through. He and other researchers quickly discovered that editing *Wikipedia* content from computers located within corporations and in government offices was widespread. Although most of the edits were innocuous—typically, individuals working on subjects unrelated to their positions—a pattern did seem to emerge of many articles being edited to reflect more favourably on the editors' hosts.

For many observers of these controversies, a troubling difference between *Wikipedia* and other encyclopaedias lies in the absence of editors and authors who will accept responsibility for the accuracy and quality of their articles. These observers point out that identifiable individuals are far easier to hold accountable for mistakes, bias, and bad writing than is a community of anonymous volunteers, but other observers respond that it is not entirely clear if there is a substantial difference. Debates about the utility of *Wikipedia* proliferated especially among scholars and educators, for whom the reliability of reference materials was of particular concern. While many classrooms, at nearly all grade levels, discouraged or prohibited students from using *Wikipedia* as a research tool, in 2010 the Wikimedia

Foundation recruited several public policy professors in the United States to develop course work wherein students contributed content to the *Wikipedia* site.

As *Wikipedia* became a seemingly inescapable part of the Internet landscape, its claims to legitimacy were further bolstered by an increasing number of citations of the encyclopaedia in U.S. judicial opinions, as well as by a program administered by the German government to work with the German-language site to improve its coverage of renewable resources. Whether or not *Wikipedia* has managed to attain the authority level of traditional encyclopaedias, it has undoubtedly become a model of what the collaborative Internet community can and cannot do.

COMPUTING IN THE CLOUD

Cloud computing is a method of running application software and storing related data in central computer systems and providing customers or other users access to them through the Internet.

EARLY DEVELOPMENT

The origin of the expression *cloud computing* is obscure, but it appears to derive from the practice of using drawings of stylized clouds to denote networks in diagrams of computing and communications systems. The term came into popular use in 2008, though the practice of providing remote access to computing functions through networks dates back to the mainframe time-sharing systems of the 1960s and 1970s. In his 1966 book *The Challenge of the Computer Utility*, the Canadian electrical engineer Douglas F. Parkhill predicted that the computer industry would come to resemble a public utility "in which many remotely located users are connected via communication links to a central computing facility."

For decades, efforts to create large-scale computer utilities were frustrated by constraints on the capacity of telecommunications networks such as the telephone system. It was cheaper and easier for companies and other organizations to store data and run applications on private computing systems maintained within their own facilities.

The constraints on network capacity began to be removed in the 1990s when telecommunications companies invested in high-capacity fibre-optic networks in response to the rapidly growing use of the Internet as a shared network for exchanging information. In the late 1990s, a number of companies, called application service providers (ASPs), were founded to supply computer applications to companies over the Internet. Most of the early ASPs failed, but their model of supplying applications remotely became popular a decade later, when it was renamed cloud computing.

CLOUD SERVICES AND MAJOR PROVIDERS

Cloud computing encompasses a number of different services. One set of services, sometimes called software as a service (SaaS), involves the supply of a discrete application to outside users. The application can be geared either to business users (such as an accounting application) or to consumers (such as an application for storing and sharing personal photographs). Another set of services, variously called utility computing, grid computing, and hardware as a service (HaaS), involves the provision of computer processing and data storage to outside users, who are able to run their own applications and store their own data on the remote system. A third set of services, sometimes called platform as a service (PaaS), involves the

Cloud computing intersects with the delivery of large amounts of data, as this sign at the 2011 EMC Corp. computing conference cleverly indicates.
Bloomberg via Getty Images

supply of remote computing capacity along with a set of software-development tools for use by outside software programmers.

Early pioneers of cloud computing include Salesforce. com, which supplies a popular business application for managing sales and marketing efforts; Google, Inc., which in addition to its search engine supplies an array of applications, known as Google Apps, to consumers and businesses; and Amazon Web Services, a division of online retailer Amazon.com, which offers access to its computing system to Web-site developers and other companies and individuals. Cloud computing also underpins popular social networks and other online media sites such as Facebook, MySpace, and Twitter. Traditional software companies, including Microsoft Corporation, Apple Inc.,

Intuit Inc., and Oracle Corporation, have also introduced cloud applications.

Cloud-computing companies either charge users for their services, through subscriptions and usage fees, or provide free access to the services and charge companies for placing advertisements in the services. Because the profitability of cloud services tends to be much lower than the profitability of selling or licensing hardware components and software programs, it is viewed as a potential threat to the businesses of many traditional computing companies.

DATA CENTRES AND PRIVACY

Construction of the large data centres that run cloud-computing services often requires investments of hundreds of millions of dollars. The centres typically contain thousands of server computers networked together into parallel-processing or grid-computing systems. The centres also often employ sophisticated virtualization technologies, which allow computer systems to be divided into many virtual machines that can be rented temporarily to customers. Because of their intensive use of electricity, the centres are often located near hydroelectric dams or other sources of cheap and plentiful electric power.

Because cloud computing involves the storage of often sensitive personal or commercial information in central database systems run by third parties, it raises concerns about data privacy and security as well as the transmission of data across national boundaries. It also stirs fears about the eventual creation of data monopolies or oligopolies. Some believe that cloud computing will, like other public utilities, come to be heavily regulated by governments.

CHAPTER 3

AN INTRUSIVE WORLD

As the tools for disseminating information have worked their way into more and more homes, so too have tools for monitoring the use of information. A society that is open to all is also a society in which all are vulnerable, creating fears that one of an individual's greatest treasures—privacy—faces threats in the Internet age that it has never faced before.

PRIVACY AND THE INTERNET

Concerns about privacy in cyberspace have become an issue of international debate. As reading and writing, health care and shopping, and sex and gossip increasingly take place in cyberspace, citizens around the world are concerned that the most intimate details of their daily lives were being monitored, searched, recorded, stored, and often misinterpreted when taken out of context. For many, the greatest threats to privacy came not from state agents but from the architecture of e-commerce itself, which was based, in unprecedented ways, on the recording and exchange of intimate personal information.

"GETTING OVER IT"

The threats to privacy in the new Internet age were crystallized in 2000 by the case of DoubleClick, Inc., the Internet's largest advertising company. For a few years DoubleClick had been compiling detailed information on the browsing habits of millions of World Wide Web users by placing "cookie" files on computer hard drives. Cookies are electronic footprints that allow Web sites and advertising networks to monitor people's online movements with telescopic precision, including the search terms people enter as well as the articles they skim and how long they spend skimming them. As long as users were confident that their virtual identities were not being linked to their actual identities, many were happy to accept DoubleClick cookies in exchange for the convenience of navigating the Web more efficiently. Then, in November 1999, DoubleClick bought Abacus Direct, which held a database of names, addresses, and information about the off-line buying habits of 90 million households compiled from the largest direct-mail catalogs and retailers in the nation. Two months later DoubleClick began compiling profiles linking individuals' actual names and addresses to Abacus's detailed records of their online and offline purchases. Suddenly, shopping that once seemed anonymous was being archived in personally identifiable dossiers.

Under pressure from privacy advocates and dot-com investors, DoubleClick announced in 2000 that it would postpone its profiling scheme until the U.S. government and the e-commerce industry had agreed on privacy standards. Two years later it settled consolidated class-action lawsuits from several states, agreeing to pay legal expenses of up to $1.8 million, to tell consumers about its data-collection activities in its online privacy policy, and to get permission before combining a consumer's personally identifiable data with his or her Web-surfing history. DoubleClick agreed to pay hundreds of thousands of dollars to settle differences with attorneys general from 10 states who were investigating its information gathering.

The retreat of DoubleClick might have seemed like a victory for privacy, but it was only an early battle in a

Kevin O'Connor, CEO of Internet advertising company DoubleClick, Inc. In 2000, DoubleClick became embroiled in controversy over profiling and privacy on the Internet. Robin London/Getty Images

much larger war—one in which many observers still worry that privacy may be vanquished. "You already have zero privacy—get over it," Scott McNealy, the CEO of Sun Microsystems, memorably remarked in 1999 in response to a question at a product show at which Sun introduced a new interactive technology called Jini. Sun's cheerful Web site promised to usher in the "networked home" of the future, in which the company's "gateway" software would operate "like a congenial party host inside the home to help consumer appliances communicate intelligently with each other and with outside networks." In this chatty new world of electronic networking, a household's refrigerator and coffeemaker could talk to a television, and all three could be monitored from the office computer. The incessant information exchanged by these gossiping appliances might, of course, generate detailed records of the most intimate details of their owners' daily lives.

New evidence seemed to emerge every day to support McNealy's grim verdict about the triumph of online surveillance technology over privacy. A survey of nearly a thousand large companies conducted by the American Management Association in 2000 found that more than half the large American firms surveyed monitored the Internet connections of their employees. Two-thirds of the firms monitored e-mail messages, computer files, or telephone conversations, up from only one-third three years earlier. Some companies used Orwellian computer software with names like Spector, Assentor, or Investigator that could monitor and record every keystroke on the computer with video-like precision. These virtual snoops could also be programmed to screen all incoming and outgoing e-mail for forbidden words and phrases—such as those involving racism, body parts, or the name of the boss—and then forward suspicious messages to a supervisor for review.

Issues in New Media

Changes in the delivery of books, music, and television have extended the technologies of surveillance beyond the office, blurring the boundaries between work and home. The same technologies that make it possible to download digitally stored books, songs, and movies directly onto computer hard drives or mobile devices could make it possible for publishers and entertainment companies to record and monitor each individual's browsing habits with unsettling specificity. Television, too, is being redesigned to create precise records of viewing habits. For instance, digital video recorders make it possible to store hours of television programs and enable viewers to skip

A customer inspects a Blackberry phone in Dubai. In 2010, the United Arab Emirates threatened a ban of Blackberry service over security concerns. AFP/ Getty Images

commercials and to create their own program lineups. However, the data generated by such actions could create viewer profiles, which could then be used to make viewing suggestions and record future shows.

Privacy of cell phone communication also has become an issue, as in 2010 when BlackBerry smartphone maker RIM reacted to demands from the United Arab Emirates (U.A.E.), Saudi Arabia, and India that security forces from those countries be given the ability to intercept communications such as e-mail and instant messages from BlackBerry users within their borders. The U.A.E. later canceled a planned ban on the BlackBerry service, saying that it had reached an agreement with RIM, which declined to reveal its discussions with the governments of

THE USA PATRIOT ACT OF 2001

In the wake of the terrorist attacks in the U.S. on Sept. 11, 2001, technology was at the forefront of international efforts to fight terrorism and bolster security. In October 2001 the administration of Pres. George W. Bush introduced, and Congress quickly passed, the Uniting and Strengthening America by Providing Appropriate Tools Required to Intercept and Obstruct Terrorism Act (the USA PATRIOT Act). The new law, aimed at empowering authorities to move more nimbly against terrorist threats, relaxed legal checks on surveillance, granting the Central Intelligence Agency (CIA) and the Federal Bureau of Investigation (FBI) a freer hand to gather data electronically on citizens and resident foreigners. The legislation also reduced the need for subpoenas, court orders, or warrants for eavesdropping on Internet communications, monitoring financial transactions, and obtaining individuals' electronic records. As part of criminal investigations, law-enforcement and intelligence agencies were authorized to track the Web sites that suspects visited and identify those to whom they sent e-mail. Internet service providers were required to turn over data on customers' Web-surfing habits to authorities on demand.

The rush to deploy new technologies and to give law-enforcement officials new investigative powers in cyberspace sparked concerns for the civil liberties of law-abiding citizens.

Civil liberties advocates worried that the PATRIOT Act's easing of judicial oversight and vague definition of legitimate subjects for electronic surveillance opened it to abuse and could cast the legal dragnet too wide in the search for incriminating evidence. The legislation paved the way for wider deployment of the controversial FBI program formerly known as Carnivore—renamed, less menacingly, DCS 1000—which sifted e-mail for particular addresses or specific text strings (sequences of characters). In December 2001 it was reported that the FBI had developed "Magic Lantern," a so-called Trojan horse program designed to crack encrypted files and e-mails. The program could implant itself surreptitiously in a suspect's computer via an e-mail message and then record keystrokes to obtain the user's passwords.

For other observers, the threat posed by religious extremists and other shadowy groups bent on mass destruction gave security precedence over freedom. Most of the law's provisions were made permanent in 2006 by the USA PATRIOT Improvement and Reauthorization

Act. In 2011 Congress extended until 2015 certain provisions desired by the administration of Pres. Barack Obama that give investigators greater latitude in wiretapping multiple telephones, surveying foreign individuals, and seizing material related to an investigation.

other countries. The demands were part of a rising tide of security demands from national governments that cited the need to monitor criminals and terrorists who used wireless communications.

The United States is not immune to these controversies. In 2010 Pres. Barack Obama's administration said that in order to prevent terrorism and identify criminals, it wanted Congress to require that all Internet services be capable of complying with wiretap orders. The broad requirement would include Internet phone services, social-networking services, and other types of Internet communication, and it would enable even encrypted messages to be decoded and read—something that required considerable time and effort. Critics complained that the monitoring proposal challenged the ideals of privacy and lack of centralized authority for which the Internet had long been known.

Photos and videos also have emerged as unexpected threats to personal privacy. "Geotags" are created when photos or videos are embedded with geographic location data from GPS chips inside cameras, including those in cell phones. When images are uploaded to the Internet, the geotags allow homes or other personal locations within the images to be precisely located by those who view the photos online. The security risk is not widely understood by the public, however, and in some cases disabling the geotag feature in certain models of digital cameras and camera-equipped smartphones is complicated.

Google's Street View photo-mapping service has caused privacy concerns since the company disclosed that it had been recording locations and some data from unprotected household wireless networks as it took pictures. The company said that the data had been gathered inadvertently. German officials objected to Google's actions on the basis of Germany's strict privacy laws, and, although German courts decided against the objections, Google did not expand its Street View service in Germany beyond the handful of urban centres that it had already photo-mapped. The controversy led to other investigations of the Street View service by several U.S. states and the governments of several countries (including the Czech Republic, which eventually refused to grant Google permission to offer the Street View service there).

Another privacy issue is cyberbullying—using the Internet to threaten or humiliate another person with words, photos, or videos. The problem received particular attention in 2010 when a male Rutgers University student committed suicide after two acquaintances reportedly streamed a video over the Internet of the student having a sexual encounter with a man. Also in 2010, Donna Witsell, the mother of a 13-year-old Florida girl who had committed suicide in 2009 after a cyberbullying incident, formed a group called Hope's Warriors to help curb abuse and to warn others of the threat. Most U.S. states have enacted laws against bullying, although very few of them include cyberbullying.

DATA MINING

Data mining is the process of discovering interesting and useful patterns and relationships in large volumes of data. The field combines tools from statistics and artificial intelligence (such as neural networks and machine learning) with database management to analyze large digital collections, known as data sets. Data mining is widely used in business (insurance, banking, retail), science research (astronomy, medicine), and government security (detection of criminals and terrorists).

The proliferation of numerous large, and sometimes connected, government and private databases has led to regulations to ensure that individual records are accurate and secure from unauthorized viewing or tampering. Most types of data mining are targeted toward ascertaining general knowledge about a group rather than knowledge about specific individuals—a supermarket is less concerned about selling one more item to one person than about selling many items to many people—though pattern analysis also may be used to discern anomalous individual behaviour such as fraud or other criminal activity.

ORIGINS AND EARLY APPLICATIONS

As computer storage capacities increased during the 1980s, many companies began to store more transactional data. The resulting record collections, often called data warehouses, were too large to be analyzed with traditional statistical approaches. Several computer science conferences and workshops were held to consider how recent advances in the field of artificial intelligence (AI)—such as discoveries from expert systems, genetic algorithms, machine learning, and neural networks—could be adapted for knowledge discovery (the preferred term in the computer science community). The process led in 1995 to the First International Conference on Knowledge Discovery and Data Mining, held in Montreal, and the launch in 1997 of the journal *Data Mining and Knowledge Discovery*. This was also the period when many early data-mining companies were formed and products were introduced.

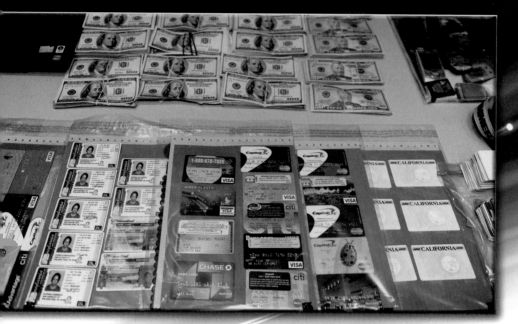

New York City police display evidence collected from a credit card and identity theft operation based in Nigeria. Data mining has proved quite useful in cracking down on credit card fraud. New York Daily News/Getty Images

One of the earliest successful applications of data mining, perhaps second only to marketing research, was credit-card-fraud detection. By studying a consumer's purchasing behaviour, a typical pattern usually becomes apparent; purchases made outside this pattern can then be flagged for later investigation or to deny a transaction. However, the wide variety of normal behaviours makes this challenging; no single distinction between normal and fraudulent behaviour works for everyone or all the time. Every individual is likely to make some purchases that differ from the types he has made before, so relying on what is normal for a single individual is likely to give too many false alarms. One approach to improving reliability is first to group individuals that have similar purchasing patterns, since group models are less sensitive to minor anomalies.

For example, a "frequent business travelers" group will likely have a pattern that includes unprecedented purchases in diverse locations, but members of this group might be flagged for other transactions, such as catalog purchases, that do not fit that group's profile.

Model Creation

The complete data-mining process involves multiple steps, from understanding the goals of a project and what data are available to implementing process changes based on the final analysis. The three key computational steps are the model-learning process, model evaluation, and use of the model. This division is clearest with classification of data. Model learning occurs when one algorithm is applied to data about which the group (or class) attribute is known in order to produce a classifier, or an algorithm learned from the data. The classifier is then tested with an independent evaluation set that contains data with known attributes. The extent to which the model's classifications agree with the known class for the target attribute can then be used to determine the expected accuracy of the model. If the model is sufficiently accurate, it can be used to classify data for which the target attribute is unknown.

Data-Mining Techniques

There are many types of data mining, typically divided by the kind of information (attributes) known and the type of knowledge sought from the data-mining model.

Predictive modeling is used when the goal is to estimate the value of a particular target attribute and there exist sample training data for which values of that attribute are known. An example is classification, which takes a set of data already divided into predefined groups and searches for patterns in the data that differentiate those groups. These discovered patterns then can be used to classify other data where the right group designation for the target attribute is unknown (though other attributes may be known). For instance, a manufacturer could develop a predictive model that distinguishes parts that fail under extreme heat, extreme cold, or other conditions based on their manufacturing environment, and this model may then be used to determine appropriate applications for each part. Another technique employed in predictive modeling is regression analysis, which can be used when the target attribute is a numeric value and the goal is to predict that value for new data.

Descriptive modeling, or clustering, also divides data into groups. With clustering, however, the proper groups are not known in advance; the patterns discovered by analyzing the data are used to determine the groups. For example, an advertiser could analyze a general population in order to classify potential customers into different clusters and then develop separate advertising campaigns targeted to each group. Fraud detection also makes use of clustering to identify groups of individuals with similar purchasing patterns.

Pattern mining concentrates on identifying rules that describe specific patterns within the data. Market-basket analysis, which identifies items that typically occur together in purchase transactions, was one of the first applications of data mining. For example, supermarkets used market-basket analysis to identify items that were often purchased together—for instance, a store featuring a fish sale would also stock up on tartar sauce. Although testing for such associations has long been feasible and is often simple to see in small data sets, data mining has enabled the discovery of less apparent associations in immense data sets. Of most interest is the discovery of unexpected associations, which may open new avenues for marketing or research. Another important use of pattern mining is the discovery of sequential patterns; for example, sequences of errors or warnings that precede an equipment failure may be used to schedule preventative maintenance or may provide insight into a design flaw.

Anomaly detection can be viewed as the flip side of clustering—that is, finding data instances that are unusual and do not fit any established pattern. Fraud detection is an example of anomaly detection. Although fraud detection may be viewed as a problem for predictive modeling, the relative rarity of fraudulent transactions and the speed with which criminals develop new types of fraud mean that any predictive model is likely to be of low accuracy and to quickly become out of date. Thus, anomaly detection instead concentrates on modeling what is normal behaviour in order to identify unusual transactions. Anomaly detection also is used with various monitoring systems, such as for intrusion detection.

Numerous other data-mining techniques have been developed, including pattern discovery in time series data (e.g., stock prices), streaming data (e.g., sensor networks), and relational learning (e.g., social networks).

Privacy Concerns and Future Directions

The potential for invasion of privacy using data mining has been a concern for many people. Commercial databases may contain detailed records of people's medical history, purchase transactions, and telephone usage, among other aspects of their lives. Civil libertarians consider some databases held by businesses and governments to be an unwarranted intrusion and an invitation to abuse. For example, the American Civil Liberties Union sued the U.S. National Security Agency (NSA) alleging warrantless spying on American citizens through the acquisition of call records from some American telecommunication companies. The program, which began in 2001, was not discovered by the public until 2006, when the information began to leak out. Often the risk is not from data mining itself (which usually aims to produce general knowledge rather than to learn information about specific issues) but from misuse or inappropriate disclosure of information in these databases.

In the United States, many federal agencies are now required to produce annual reports that specifically address the privacy implications of their data-mining projects. The U.S. law requiring privacy reports from federal

Citizens attend a 2008 press conference to discuss alleged spying by state police in Maryland. The press conference was held at the ACLU of Maryland headquarters. Baltimore Sun/McClatchy-Tribune/Getty Images

agencies defines data mining quite restrictively as "...analyses to discover or locate a predictive pattern or anomaly indicative of terrorist or criminal activity on the part of any individual or individuals." As various local, national, and international law-enforcement agencies have begun to share or integrate their databases, the potential for abuse or security breaches has forced governments to work with industry on developing more secure computers and networks. In particular, there has been research in techniques for privacy-preserving data mining that operate on distorted, transformed, or encrypted data to decrease the risk of disclosure of any individual's data.

Data mining is evolving, with one driver being competitions on challenge problems. A commercial example of this was the $1 million Netflix Prize. Netflix, an American company that offers movie rentals delivered by mail or streamed over the Internet, began the contest in 2006 to see if anyone could improve by 10 percent its recommendation system, an algorithm for predicting an individual's movie preferences based on previous rental data. The prize was awarded on Sept. 21, 2009, to BellKor's Pragmatic Chaos—a team of seven mathematicians, computer scientists, and engineers from the United States, Canada, Austria, and Israel who had achieved the 10 percent goal on June 26, 2009, and finalized their victory with an improved algorithm 30 days later. The three-year open competition had spurred many clever data-mining innovations from contestants. For example, the 2007 and 2008 Conferences on Knowledge Discovery and Data Mining held workshops on the Netflix Prize, at which research papers were presented on topics ranging from new collaborative filtering techniques to faster matrix factorization (a key component of many recommendation systems). Concerns over privacy of such data have also led to advances in understanding privacy and anonymity.

Winners of the 2009 Netflix Prize. The $1 million award is given to the person or team that devises a data-mining algorithm that improves Netflix's recommendation system by at least 10 percent. Jason Kempin/Getty Images

Data mining is not a panacea, however, and results must be viewed with the same care as with any statistical analysis. One of the strengths of data mining is the ability to analyze quantities of data that would be impractical to analyze manually, and the patterns found may be complex and difficult for humans to understand; this complexity requires care in evaluating the patterns. Nevertheless, statistical evaluation techniques can result in knowledge that is free from human bias, and the large amount of data can reduce biases inherent in smaller samples. Used properly, data mining provides valuable insights into large data sets that otherwise would not be practical or possible to obtain.

CHAPTER 4

A TROUBLED WORLD

Even more serious than the erosion of privacy in cyber-space is an individual's vulnerability to new forms of crime. In addition, the tools of free information exchange have forced society to reconsider long-accepted notions of intellectual property. Even as vulnerability to cyber-crime is a worry, some dividing lines between what is legal and what is illegal seem to be shifting.

CYBERCRIME

Cybercrime is the use of a computer as an instrument to further illegal ends, such as committing fraud, trafficking in child pornography and intellectual property, stealing identities, or violating privacy. Cybercrime, especially through the Internet, has grown in importance as the computer has become central to commerce, entertainment, and government. Hardly a hamlet in the world has not been touched by cybercrime of one sort or another.

DEFINING CYBERCRIME

New technologies create new criminal opportunities but few new types of crime. What distinguishes cybercrime from traditional criminal activity? Obviously, one difference is the use of the digital computer, but technology alone is insufficient for any distinction that might exist between different realms of criminal activity. Criminals do not need a computer to commit fraud, traffic in child pornography and intellectual property, steal an identity, or violate someone's privacy. All those activities existed before the "cyber" prefix became ubiquitous. Cybercrime, especially involving the Internet, represents an extension of existing criminal behaviour alongside some novel illegal activities.

Most cybercrime is an attack on information about individuals, corporations, or governments. Although the attacks do not take place on a physical body, they do take place on the personal or corporate virtual body, which is the set of informational attributes that define people and institutions on the Internet. In other words, in the digital age our virtual identities are essential elements of everyday life: we are a bundle of numbers and identifiers in multiple computer databases owned by governments and corporations. Cybercrime highlights the centrality of networked computers in our lives, as well as the fragility of such seemingly solid facts as individual identity.

An important aspect of cybercrime is its nonlocal character; actions can occur in jurisdictions separated by vast distances. This poses severe problems for law enforcement since previously local or even national crimes now require international cooperation. For example, if a person accesses child pornography located on a computer in a country that does not ban child pornography, is that individual committing a crime in a nation where such materials are illegal? Where exactly does cybercrime take place? Cyberspace is simply a richer version of the space where a telephone conversation takes place, somewhere between the two people having the conversation. As a planet-spanning network, the Internet offers criminals multiple hiding places in the real world as well as in the network itself. However, just as individuals walking on the ground leave marks that a skilled tracker can follow, cybercriminals leave clues as to their identity and location, despite their best efforts to cover their tracks. In order to follow such clues across national boundaries, though, international cybercrime treaties must be ratified.

In 1996 the Council of Europe, together with government representatives from the United States, Canada, and Japan, drafted a preliminary international treaty covering computer crime. Around the world, civil libertarian groups immediately protested provisions in the treaty requiring Internet service providers (ISPs) to store information on their customers' transactions and to turn this information over on demand. Work on the treaty proceeded nevertheless, and on Nov. 23, 2001, the Council of Europe Cybercrime Convention was signed by 30 states. Additional protocols, covering terrorist activities and racist and xenophobic cybercrimes, were proposed in 2002. In addition, various national laws, such as the USA PATRIOT Act of 2001, have expanded law enforcement's power to monitor and protect computer networks.

Cybercrime ranges across a spectrum of activities. At one end are crimes that involve fundamental breaches of personal or corporate privacy, such as assaults on the integrity of information held in digital depositories and the use of illegally obtained digital information to blackmail a firm or individual. Also at this end of the spectrum is the crime of identity theft. Midway along the spectrum lie transaction-based crimes such as fraud, trafficking in child pornography, digital piracy, money laundering, and counterfeiting. These are specific crimes with specific victims, but the criminal hides in the relative anonymity provided by the Internet. Another part of this type of crime involves individuals within corporations or government bureaucracies deliberately altering data for either profit or political objectives.

A policeman in Fort Lauderdale, Fla., poses as a young girl in an online chat room to help identify and arrest child predators on the Internet. Joe Raedle/ Getty Images

At the other end of the spectrum are those crimes that involve attempts to disrupt the actual workings of the Internet. These range from spam, hacking, and denial of service attacks against specific sites to acts of cyberterrorism—that is, the use of the Internet to cause public disturbances and even death. Cyberterrorism focuses upon the use of the Internet by nonstate actors to affect a nation's economic and technological infrastructure. Since the September 11 attacks of 2001, public awareness of the threat of cyberterrorism has grown dramatically.

IDENTITY THEFT

Cybercrime affects both a virtual and a real body, but the effects upon each are different. This phenomenon is clearest in the case of identity theft. In the United States, for example, individuals do not have an official identity card but a Social Security number that has long served as a de facto identification number. Taxes are collected on the basis of each citizen's Social Security number, and many private institutions use the number to keep track of their employees, students, and patients. Access to an individual's Social Security number affords the opportunity to gather all the documents related to that person's citizenship—i.e., to steal his identity.

Even stolen credit card information can be used to reconstruct an individual's identity. When criminals steal a firm's credit card records, they produce two distinct effects. First, they make off with digital information about individuals that is useful in many ways. For example, they might use the credit card information to run up huge bills, forcing the credit card firms to suffer large losses, or they might sell the information to others who can use it in a similar fashion. Second, they might use individual credit card names and numbers to create new identities for other criminals. For example, a criminal might contact the issuing bank of a stolen credit card and change the mailing address on the account. Next, the criminal may get a passport or driver's license with his own picture but with the victim's name. With a driver's license, the criminal can easily acquire a new Social Security card; it is then possible to open bank accounts and receive loans—all with the victim's credit record and background. The original cardholder might remain unaware of this until the debt is so great that the bank contacts the account holder. Only then does the identity theft become visible.

Although identity theft takes places in many countries, researchers and law-enforcement officials are plagued by a lack of information and statistics about the crime worldwide. Interpol, the international policing agency, has not

Protect yourself with these easy steps:

Don't leave mail in your mailbox overnight or on weekends.

Deposit mail in U.S. Postal Service collection boxes.

Tear up unwanted documents that contain personal information.

Review your consumer credit report annually.

When Bad Things Happen
To Your Good Name

For more information on identity theft, visit

www.usps.com/postalinspectors

If you are a victim, call the ID Theft hotline at **1-877-987-3728**

A poster warning residents of Portland, Maine, about the dangers of identity theft. © AP Images

added any type of cybercrime, including identity theft, to its annual crime statistics. Cybercrime is clearly, however, an international problem.

In 2003 the U.S. Federal Trade Commission (FTC) released the first national survey on identity theft; according to the report, in the previous year 3.3 million Americans had their identities fraudulently used to open bank, credit card, or utility accounts, with losses of $32.9 billion to businesses and $3.8 billion to individuals. The report also stated that another 6.6 million Americans were victimized by account theft, such as use of stolen credit cards and automatic teller machine (ATM) cards, with losses of $14 billion to businesses and $1.1 billion to individuals. The annual FTC reports show that the total number of identity theft victims in the United States has declined in each subsequent year, reaching about 250,000 in 2010, but the average loss incurred by individuals and businesses per incident has grown enough to keep the total losses near $50 billion every year.

HACKING AND DENIAL OF SERVICE ATTACKS

While breaching privacy to detect cybercrime works well when the crimes involve the theft and misuse of information, ranging from credit card numbers and personal data to file sharing of various commodities—music, video, or child pornography—what of crimes that attempt to wreak havoc on the very workings of the machines that make up the network? The story of hacking actually goes back to the 1950s, when a group of phreaks (short for "phone freaks") began to hijack portions of the world's telephone networks, making unauthorized long-distance calls and setting up special "party lines" for fellow phreaks. With the proliferation of computer bulletin board systems (BBSs)

PHISHING

Phishing is the act of sending e-mail that purports to be from a reputable source, such as the recipient's bank or credit card provider, and that seeks to acquire personal or financial information. The name derives from the idea of "fishing" for information.

In phishing, typically a fraudulent e-mail message is used to direct a potential victim to a World Wide Web site that mimics the appearance of a familiar bank or e-commerce site. The person is then asked to "update" or "confirm" their accounts, thereby unwittingly disclosing confidential information such as their Social Security number or a credit-card number. In addition to or instead of directly defrauding a victim, this information may be used by criminals to perpetrate identity theft, which may not be discovered for many years.

In 2007, according to Gartner, Inc., an American technology research company, 8.5 billion phishing e-mails were sent out globally each month, the total number of victims for the year was about 3.2 million, and their losses were in excess of $3.6 billion. These figures have remained largely stable in subsequent years.

in the late 1970s, the informal phreaking culture began to coalesce into quasi-organized groups of individuals who graduated from the telephone network to "hacking" corporate and government computer network systems.

Although the term *hacker* predates computers and was used as early as the mid-1950s in connection with electronic hobbyists, the first recorded instance of its use in connection with computer programmers who were adept at writing, or "hacking," computer code seems to have been in a 1963 article in a student newspaper at the Massachusetts Institute of Technology (MIT). After the first computer systems were linked to multiple users through telephone lines in the early 1960s, *hacker* came to refer to individuals who gained unauthorized access to computer networks, whether from another computer network or, as personal computers became available, from their own computer systems.

When discussing hacker culture, it is interesting to note that most hackers have not been criminals in the sense of being vandals or seeking illicit financial rewards. Instead, most have been young people driven by intellectual curiosity; many of these people have gone on to become computer security architects. However, as some hackers sought notoriety among their peers, their exploits led to clear-cut crimes. In particular, hackers began breaking into computer systems and then bragging to one another about their exploits, sharing pilfered documents as trophies to prove their boasts. These exploits grew as

hackers not only broke into but sometimes took control of government and corporate computer networks.

One such criminal was Kevin Mitnick, the first hacker to make the "most wanted list" of the U.S. Federal Bureau of Investigation (FBI). He allegedly broke into the North American Aerospace Defense Command (NORAD) computer in 1981, when he was 17 years old, a feat that brought to the fore the gravity of the threat posed by such security breaches. In 1988 the Internet played a role only in the lives of researchers and academics; by 2000 it had become essential to the workings of the U.S. government and economy. Cybercrime had moved from being an issue of individual wrongdoing to being a matter of national security.

Concern with hacking contributed first to an overhaul of federal sentencing in the United States, with the 1984 Comprehensive Crime Control Act, and then with the Computer Fraud and Abuse Act of 1986. The scale of hacking crimes is among the most difficult to assess because the victims often prefer not to report the crimes, sometimes out of embarrassment or fear of further security breaches. Officials estimate, however, that hacking costs the world economy billions of dollars annually.

Hacking is not always an outside job. A related criminal endeavour involves individuals within corporations or government bureaucracies deliberately altering database records for either profit or political objectives. The greatest losses stem from the theft of proprietary information, sometimes followed up by the extortion of money from the original owner for the data's return. In this sense, hacking is old-fashioned industrial espionage by other means.

was discovered by researchers at the University of Toronto, who had been asked by representatives of the Dalai Lama to investigate the exiled Tibetan leader's computers for possible malware. In addition to finding out that the Dalai Lama's computers were compromised, the researchers discovered that GhostNet had infiltrated more than a thousand computers around the world. The highest concentration of compromised systems were within embassies and foreign affairs bureaus of or located in South Asian and Southeast Asian countries. Reportedly, the computers were infected by users who opened e-mail attachments or clicked on Web page links. Once infected with the GhostNet malware, the computers began "phishing" for files throughout the local network—even turning on cameras and video-recording devices for remote monitoring. Three control servers that ran the malware were located in Hainan, Guangdong, and Sichuan provinces in China, and a fourth server was located in California.

Compare Mitnick's 1981 hack with the events of the week of Feb. 7, 2000, when "mafiaboy," a 15-year-old Canadian hacker, orchestrated a series of denial of service (DoS) attacks against several e-commerce sites, including Amazon.com and eBay.com. These attacks used computers at multiple locations to overwhelm the vendors' computers and shut down their Web sites to legitimate commercial traffic. The attacks crippled Internet commerce, with the FBI estimating that the affected sites suffered $1.7 billion in damages.

Distributed DoS attacks are a special kind of hacking. A criminal salts an array of computers with computer programs that can be triggered by an external computer user. These programs are known as Trojan horses, since they enter the unknowing users' computers as something benign, such as a photo or document attached to an e-mail. At a predesignated time, this Trojan horse program begins to send messages to a predetermined site. If enough computers have been compromised, it is likely that the selected site can be tied up so effectively that little if any legitimate traffic can reach it.

One important insight offered by these events has been that much software is insecure, making it easy for even an unskilled hacker to compromise a vast number of machines. Although software companies regularly offer patches to fix software vulnerabilities, not all users implement the updates, and their computers remain vulnerable to criminals wanting to launch DoS attacks. In 2003 the Internet service provider PSINet Europe connected an unprotected server to the Internet. Within 24 hours the server had been attacked 467 times, and after three weeks more than 600 attacks had been recorded. Only vigorous security regimes can protect against such an environment. Despite the claims about the pacific nature of the Internet, it is best to think of it as a modern example of the Wild West of American lore—with the sheriff far away.

SPAM

E-mail has spawned one of the most significant forms of cybercrime—spam, or unsolicited advertisements for products and services, which experts estimate to make up as much as 90 percent of the e-mail circulating on the Internet. Although e-mail is the most common means of transmitting spam, blogs, social networking sites, newsgroups, and cellular telephones are also targeted. Viewed with widespread disdain, spam is considered a crime against all users of the Internet since it wastes both the storage and network capacities of ISPs, as well as often simply being offensive. Yet, despite various attempts to legislate it out of existence, it remains unclear how spam

A screen shot of a computer e-mail in-box filled with unwanted spam messages. Spam is more than simply annoying. It also monopolizes space on Internet Service Provider servers and networks. Mike Clarke/AFP/Getty Images

can be eliminated without violating the freedom of speech in a liberal democratic polity. Unlike junk mail, which has a postage cost associated with it, spam is nearly free for perpetrators—it typically costs the same to send 10 messages as it does to send 10 million.

The origin of spam dates to 1978, when Gary Thuerk, a marketing manager for the now defunct computer company Digital Equipment Corporation, sent out an unsolicited mass e-mail promoting his firm's computer products. Sent to hundreds of computers over ARPANET, Thuerk's message immediately provoked ire among the recipients and a reprimand from the network's administrators. Thuerk's e-mail is now widely credited as the first example of spam, although the term was not used to refer to unsolicited mass e-mails until many years later. (The inspiration for using the term is believed to be a 1970s *Monty Python's Flying Circus* television sketch in which a group of Vikings sing a chorus about Spam, a processed meat product, that drowns out all other conversation at a restaurant.)

The commercial potential of spam grew along with the popularity of the Internet. In 1994 American lawyers Laurence Canter and Martha Siegel flooded USENET's discussion groups with a message offering legal services to immigrants who were applying for U.S. green cards. The mass posting provoked outrage, but the tactic brought in more than $100,000 in revenue, and the modern spam industry was born.

Initially, most spam featured unsolicited offers from businesses that made no attempt to hide their identity. Eventually, spammers (those who send spam) went underground and began to hide their identity and location, and the content of spam became more nefarious, often advertising pornography or promoting various scams. In addition to offensive content, spam may contain viruses and malicious software (called malware) that can invade a recipient's computer, allowing spammers to gain remote access to the computer. Compromised computers (called zombies) can be linked together to form a network of computers (called a botnet) that is surreptitiously controlled by the spammer and used to distribute spam or to commit a variety of cybercrimes.

Some jurisdictions have taken legal action against spammers. However, lack of consistent international legal standards and the desire to protect free speech make legislative solutions difficult. Filtering software is used to block much of the spam that is sent, although spammers have become adept at coming up with new techniques to bypass security filters, making it necessary for filtering software to constantly evolve.

MALWARE

Malware, or "*mal*icious soft*ware*," is any kind of malicious computer program, such as a virus, trojan, spyware, or worm. Malware typically infects a personal computer (PC) through e-mail, Web sites, or attached hardware devices.

Malware may be used to take over PCs, turning them into zombie computers that may form part of a "botnet" used to send out spam or perform denial of service attacks on Web sites. In addition, malware has been used to distribute pornography and unlicensed software. Owners of infected PCs often become aware of a problem only as their machines become progressively slower or they find unidentifiable software that cannot be removed.

The deliberate release of damaging computer software was the crime of choice of the first person to be convicted in the United States under the Computer Fraud and Abuse Act of 1986. On Nov. 2, 1988, a computer science student at Cornell University named Robert Morris released a software "worm" onto the Internet from MIT (as a guest on the campus, he hoped to remain anonymous). The worm was an experimental self-propagating and replicating computer program that took advantage of flaws in certain e-mail protocols. Due to a mistake in its programming, rather than just sending copies of itself to other computers, this software kept replicating itself on each infected system, filling all the available computer memory. Before a fix was found, the worm had brought some 6,000 computers (one-tenth of the Internet) to a halt.

Although Morris's worm cost time and millions of dollars to fix, the event had few commercial consequences, for the Internet had not yet become a fixture of economic affairs. That Morris's father was the head of computer security for the U.S. National Security Agency led the press to treat the event more as a high-tech Oedipal drama than as a foreshadowing of things to come. Since then, ever more harmful viruses have been cooked up by political activists and misfits from locations as diverse as the United States, Bulgaria, Pakistan, and the Philippines.

Malware development has kept pace with increasingly sophisticated malware detection and prevention software. Most commercial antivirus software programs include features to help detect and eliminate malware. In addition, modern operating systems include features to make it harder for criminals to install malware without the owners' knowledge. Still, all such preventative measures are ineffective if users do not regularly update their system and antivirus software, and no combination of security measures will work if individuals indulge in imprudent behaviour.

The evolution of malware reached a new milestone in 2010, when the Stuxnet worm proliferated on computers around the world. Characterized as "weaponized software" by security experts, Stuxnet exploited four separate vulnerabilities in the Windows operating system to achieve administrator-level control over specialized industrial networks created by Siemens AG. By attacking these supervisory control and data acquisition (SCADA) systems, Stuxnet was able to cause industrial processes

Subject

OOC   Re: applicati

OOC   ILOVEYOU

OOC   ILOVEYOU

OOC   ILOVEYOU

OOC   ILOVEYOU

OOC   ILOVEYOU

Malware such as the "I Love You" virus, unleashed globally in 2000, is designed to wreak havoc on personal computers, slowing them down or wiping out information altogether. © AP Images

to behave in a manner inconsistent with their original programming, thus crossing the line between cyberspace and the "real world." Stuxnet's intended target seems to have been nuclear installations in Iran, raising speculation that the worm may have been a sophisticated cyberattack mounted by either the United States or Israel or both. In any case the worm demonstrated that critical infrastructure sites as nuclear power plants and electrical grid substations could be subverted by malicious code.

Viruses, Worms, Trojans, and Spyware

A computer virus is a portion of a program code that has been designed to furtively copy itself into other such codes or computer files. It is usually created by a prankster or vandal to effect a nonutilitarian result or to destroy data and program code.

A virus consists of a set of instructions that attaches itself to other computer programs, usually in the computer's operating system, and becomes part of them. In most cases, the corrupted programs continue to perform their intended functions but surreptitiously execute the virus's instructions as well. A virus is usually designed to execute when it is loaded into a computer's memory. Upon execution, the virus instructs its host program to copy the viral code into, or "infect," any number of other programs and files stored in the computer. The infection can then transfer itself to files and code on other computers through magnetic disks or other memory-storage devices, computer networks, or online systems. The replicating viruses often multiply until they destroy data or render other program codes meaningless. A virus may simply cause a harmless joke or cryptic message to appear on a computer user's video monitor each time he turns on his computer. A more damaging virus can wreak havoc on an extremely large computer system within a matter of minutes or hours, causing it to crash and thereby destroy valuable data.

A computer worm is a program designed to furtively copy itself into other computers. Unlike a computer virus, which "infects" other programs in order to transmit itself to still more programs, worms are generally independent programs and need no "host." In fact, worms typically need no human action to replicate across networks. Whereas the first worm outbreaks, such as Robert Morris's 1988 attack, were typically pranks and relatively benign, cybercriminals began using them to create zombie computers, linked by the millions in botnets, that were activated to send out spam, often for hire, or to flood Web sites with denial-of-service attacks, often involving blackmail schemes.

A trojan, or Trojan horse virus, is a type of malware disguised within legitimate or beneficial programs or files. Once installed on a user's computer system, the trojan allows the malware developer remote access to the host computer, subjecting the host computer to a variety of destructive or undesired activities. Named for the Trojan horse, the famed act of subterfuge that enabled the ancient Greeks to capture the city of Troy, computer trojans can pose a serious threat to unsuspecting computer users. The user first unknowingly installs the trojan application, usually spread through instant-messaging software, e-mail attachments, or Web downloads. Through activation of this "backdoor" access, the computer becomes a zombie, allowing a remote malware user to perform any action that the computer owner could on the infected computer. Thousands of trojans in circulation are used for a variety of malicious purposes: browsing the hard drive to steal data, logging key strokes to acquire personal passwords or account numbers, erasing files, shutting down the computer at random, sending spam from the user's e-mail account, or deleting the entire hard drive.

Trojans can affect millions of computers simultaneously, and they are sometimes used in targeted attacks against the networks of government organizations, universities, or businesses. They are frequently used for illegal activity such as corporate espionage, blackmail, fraud, and identity theft, but relatively few of those responsible have been identified and prosecuted. Trojans and other malware were developed alongside the personal computer, with the first trojans theorized in the early 1980s and developed in the 1990s

Spyware is a type of program that is secretly installed on a person's computer in order to divulge the owner's private information, including lists of Web sites visited and passwords and credit-card numbers input, via the Internet. Some spyware is designed to steal U.S. Social Security numbers, passwords, and other private information directly from an infected computer's hard drive, while other spyware may alter the results of Internet searches in order to redirect users to a Web site that may infect their computers with even more spyware. Spyware typically finds its way onto users' computers when they install some other software, such as electronic games or system utilities, from third-party sources that have altered the original programs. For example, a large proportion of software downloaded from P2P ("person-to-person") file-sharing networks contains computer viruses, worms, spyware, adware (unsolicited advertisements), or other malware. Spyware may also be secretly installed when a user opens an infected e-mail attachment. Because digital audio or video files are frequently shared among friends, a contaminated file can quickly proliferate if left unchecked.

ROOTKITS

Rootkits are one of the worst forms of malware. Their name comes from the fact that they infect the "root-level" of a computer's hard drive, making them impossible to remove without completely erasing the drives. Typically, a PC becomes infected with a rootkit when the owner installs some software obtained over the Internet, especially copyrighted software that has been distributed illegally. Infected computers are often used by cybercriminals for the distribution of spam and pornography.

In efforts to curb copyright infringement, some computer software makers and music companies secretly install detection software on users' machines. For example, it was revealed in 2005 that the Sony Corporation had been secretly installing rootkits as its music CDs were loaded into PCs. The rootkit was discovered because of the way that it collected information on users' PCs and sent the data back to Sony. The revelation turned into a public relations disaster, which forced the company to abandon the practice. The practice of monitoring users' data, with or without installing rootkits, continues in the software industry.

ZOMBIES AND BOTNETS

A zombie is a computer connected to the Internet that has been taken over by a computer worm, virus, or other malware. Groups of such machines, called botnets (from a combination of *robot* and *network*), often carry out criminal actions without their owners' detecting any unusual activity. Over time, however, most zombie computers accumulate so much malware that they become unusable by their owners. Often, the only cure for heavily infected machines is to completely erase the hard drive and reinstall the operating system. There are millions of zombie computers in the world, about one-fourth of them located in the United States.

The most typical use of botnets is for widely disseminating spam (unwanted commercial e-mail), which makes it difficult to determine the original spammer. Cybercrime experts believe that 50 percent to 80 percent of all spam is generated by botnets. Similarly, botnets are used to transmit phishing scams, which seek to extract personal data from unwary individuals. Occasionally, botnets are used to launch denial of service attacks on Web sites, effectively shutting them down. Although criminals have sometimes tried to extort money from Web site administrators with threats of continual denial of service attacks, such attacks more often are based on some political, environmental, or religious motivation.

Individual zombie computers have been used to store and transmit child pornography and other illegal materials, which has sometimes resulted in the prosecution of individuals, including minors, who are later shown to be innocent. In an effort to combat botnets, some computer security scientists, such as those associated with the German Honeynet Project, have begun creating fake zombies, which can enter into and interact with members of a botnet in order to intercept commands relayed by their operators. This information can then be used to help find and arrest the "masterminds."

The scale of botnets can be illustrated by a particularly large operation uncovered in April 2009. A six-person gang operating out of Ukraine had compromised 1.9 million computers around the world; approximately half were in the United States. The cybercriminals infected others' computers using JavaScript code executed within a Web browser to install a trojan that they could activate on command. The criminals were discovered after they posted an advertisement on a criminal "black-hat" site offering to rent out portions of their botnet.

FILE SHARING AND PIRACY

Piracy is the act of illegally reproducing or disseminating copyrighted material, such as computer programs, books, music, and films. Although any form of copyright infringement can and has been referred to as piracy, this section of this chapter focuses on using computers to make digital copies of works for distribution over the Internet.

One of the most troublesome areas of piracy is the distribution of music copied from compact discs (CDs),

Napster founder Shawn Fanning speaks to the press after an appeals court upheld an earlier verdict that the company was guilty of copyright infringement. Napster was shut down shortly thereafter. John G. Mabanglo/AFP/ Getty Images

which are the major source of revenue for recording companies. Although piracy has always been a problem, especially in the Far East, the proliferation on college campuses of inexpensive personal computers capable of capturing music off CDs and sharing them over high-speed ("broadband") Internet connections has become the recording industry's greatest nightmare.

In one of the most celebrated cases of copyright enforcement in the United States, the recording industry, represented by the Recording Industry Association of America (RIAA), attacked a single file-sharing service, Napster, which from 1999 to 2001 allowed users across the Internet access to music files, stored in the data-compression format known as MP3, on other users' computers by way of Napster's central computer. According to the RIAA, Napster users regularly violated the copyright of recording artists, and the service had to stop. For users, the issues were not so clear-cut. At the core of the Napster case was the issue of fair use. Individuals who had purchased a CD were clearly allowed to listen to the music, whether in their home stereo, automobile sound system, or personal computer. What they did not have the right to do, argued the RIAA, was to make the CD available to thousands of others who could make a perfect digital copy of the music and create their own CDs. Users rejoined that sharing their files was a fair use of copyrighted material for which they had paid a fair price. In the end, the RIAA argued that a whole new class of cybercriminal had been born—the digital pirate—that included just about anyone who had ever shared or downloaded an MP3 file.

Although the RIAA successfully shuttered Napster in 2001 (the name would later be resurrected for a legitimate e-commerce Web site), a new type of file-sharing service, known as peer-to-peer (P2P) networks, sprang up. These decentralized systems do not rely on a central facilitating computer; instead, they consist of millions of users who voluntarily open their own computers to others for file sharing. The RIAA continues to battle these file-sharing networks, demanding that ISPs turn over records of their customers who move large quantities of data over their networks, but the effects have been minimal. The RIAA's other tactic has been to push for the development of technologies to enforce the digital rights of copyright holders. So-called digital rights management (DRM) technology is an attempt to forestall piracy through technologies that will not allow consumers to share files or possess "too many" copies of a copyrighted work.

As companies work on the hardware and software necessary to meet these goals, it is clear that file sharing has brought about a fundamental reconstruction of the relationship between producers, distributors, and consumers of artistic material. As broadband Internet connections proliferate, the motion-picture industry faces a similar problem, although optical discs in DVD and Blu-ray formats have come to market with increasingly sophisticated encryption and various built-in attempts to avoid the problems of a video Napster.

Meanwhile, copyright owners have begun accommodating themselves with the idea of commercial digital distribution. Examples include the online sales by the iTunes Store (run by Apple Inc.) and Amazon.com of music, television shows, and movies in downloadable formats, with and without DRM restrictions. In addition, several cable and satellite television providers, as well as many electronic game systems (Sony Corporation's PlayStation 3 and Microsoft Corporation's Xbox 360), have developed "video-on-demand" services that allow customers to download movies and shows for immediate (streaming) or later playback.

From Hackers to Pirates

Before PCs and the digital age, most individuals did not have the capability to copy works in order to print books, press vinyl records, or burn film—nor did they have the ability to distribute copies beyond their immediate circle of family and friends. As a practical matter, copyright law and its enforcement was historically concerned with preventing those with publishing equipment, such as a printing press, from unlicensed reproduction and distribution of copyrighted material for profit.

A certain acceptance or disregard of software piracy, or "code sharing," had been fostered among "hackers," or early computer programmers, in the academic computer science laboratories of the 1950s and '60s. Apple Computers (now Apple Inc.) famously even flew a Jolly Roger flag (a flag with the traditional pirate emblem of a skull and crossbones) on its corporate campus for more than a year starting in 1983. Similarly, during a candid moment in front of an audience at the University of Washington in 1998, Microsoft cofounder Bill Gates acknowledged the problem with enforcing software copyrights in the developing world:

> *Although about 3 million computers get sold every year in China, people don't pay for the software. Someday they will, though, and as long as they're going to steal it, we want them to steal ours. They'll get sort of addicted, and then we'll somehow figure out how to collect sometime in the next decade.*

MP3 and P2P Networks

The piracy situation began to change with the creation of the Internet and its opening to the public in the

THE PIRATE BAY

The Pirate Bay is a file-sharing Web site founded in 2003 by the Swedish anticopyright group Piratbyrån ("Bureau of Piracy"). The Pirate Bay is the most popular site in the world to use the BitTorrent protocol that allows the distribution of very large files such as those containing movies and electronic games. The site is an enthusiastic defender of information piracy and is often the target of legal complaints from music companies, movie studios, and other content providers whose works can be found there.

The Pirate Bay allows the sharing of audio, video, software, and electronic games, with newly released movies and recently transmitted television programs being the most popular content. The site does not host any files itself but only the information about where to find files. The files themselves are distributed among the users of The Pirate Bay site. Files are shared using the BitTorrent protocol in which files are divided into smaller pieces, distributed among various users, and then reassembled. The Pirate Bay originally hosted a torrent tracker that recorded where the files resided. However, since November 2009 The Pirate Bay has used a system called magnet links, in which files are assigned values for which a user can then search. Thus, The Pirate Bay has no record of where the files are located.

When presented with legal notices of copyright infringement to remove materials from their Web site, the operators of The Pirate Bay sometimes posted these notices on their Web site and responded with ridicule and contempt, claiming that they were operating in accordance with Swedish law (and thus antipiracy laws such as the U.S. Digital Millennium Copyright Act did not apply) and that the very nature of file-sharing technology meant that there were no materials to be removed. The Pirate Bay has also defended itself against claims that it profits from piracy by noting that it does not charge users for its services and relies on advertising on the site for revenue.

In 2004 The Pirate Bay became independent from Piratbyrån. In May 2006 the Swedish police raided PRQ, the Internet service provider that hosted The Pirate Bay, and confiscated several servers. The raid shut down the Web site but only for three days. In January 2008 the operators of The Pirate Bay, Frederik Neij, Gottfrid Svartholm, and Peter Sunde, and businessman Carl Lundström, who had supplied servers and bandwidth to the site, were charged with copyright infringement, and in April 2009 they were sentenced to one year in prison and the payment of a fine of 30 million kronor ($3.6 million). In November 2010 the jail terms of Neij, Sunde, and Lundström were reduced upon appeal; however, their fine was increased to 46 million kronor ($6.6 million). (Svartholm was ill at the time, and his appeal was postponed.) The Web site continued in operation, receiving about three million visitors per day.

mid-1990s. In particular, the change from piracy-as-a-business to piracy-as-a-hobby started with the invention and widespread dissemination of software for creating music in the MP3, or MPEG-1 Audio Layer 3, format. The MP3 was designed in the early 1990s by engineers in the international Moving Picture Experts Group (MPEG). Their goal was to create a data compression format that would result in digital versions of analog music, thereby requiring much less storage space without substantially degrading the sound quality. For example, a typical three-minute song might occupy about 50 megabytes (MB) of computer space in analog form (as used on a regular record or CD) but its MP3 form a mere 4 MB or so, depending on the sampling rate (higher sampling rates produce better quality but require more storage space). Individuals quickly discovered that songs in MP3 format could be exchanged in only a few minutes over the Internet, even with the slower modems available in the 1990s.

This, in turn, led to the development of file-sharing networks such as Napster, which relied on P2P software for distributing songs. Although the Recording Industry Association of America (RIAA) succeeded in shutting down Napster, which had facilitated billions of song transfers over the Internet from 1999 to 2001, newer P2P programs became available that no longer required a central server for indexing song locations. Nevertheless, various computers were soon set up to facilitate searches, the most infamous being The Pirate Bay, a Swedish service that began tracking BitTorrent files (a common P2P format) across BitTorrent servers in 2003.

Some music recording artists have taken the view that piracy helps sell their backlist of works long after their publishers have stopped promoting them. For example, Janis Ian, an American Grammy Award winner, wrote a famous essay in 2002 about her experiences with increased sales of her songs after MP3 versions began circulating around the Internet.

FILM AND DRM

With the experience of the RIAA as a guide, the Motion Picture Association of America (MPAA) campaigned for digital rights management (DRM) software to be included in DVDs, DVD players, and the HDMI (High-Definition Multimedia Interface) standard for connecting modern home theatre components. The MPAA's task of combating piracy was helped by the vastly larger size of motion picture files, which require much more computing power and time for conversion and distribution over the Internet, even with broadband connections. Most digital video recorders (DVRs), as supplied by cable and satellite television providers, also have DRM software to prevent recorded material from being moved to other devices, or data encryption is used to prevent the material from being viewed on other devices or converted to other formats for further distribution. The inclusion of DRM software has encouraged the commercial distribution, for sale or rent, of movies and television shows through DVRs and electronic game consoles from Microsoft (Xbox 360) and the Sony Corporation (PlayStation 3).

Of course, no DRM scheme is foolproof, and there exist modern-day hackers around the world with computer programming skills and relentless determination to share videos via P2P networks. The difficulty in stopping people from viewing what they want to view, when they want to view it, no doubt contributed to movie and television studios' deciding to offer their products to consumers at Web sites where they could include advertisements. In particular, viewers at such advertiser-supported sites are assured that their machines will not become infected with malware embedded within the media, and the producers gain another source of income that they hope will grow enough to eventually compensate for the additional cost of distribution over the Internet.

E-BOOKS AND PROMOTIONAL PIRACY

Whereas many electronic books, or e-books, existed for years for works that had passed into the public domain, the requirement of reading them on a computer limited their appeal for many years. Even best sellers, such as J.K. Rowling's *Harry Potter and the Order of the Phoenix* (2003), which was scanned and uploaded to the Internet within hours of its publication, had a minuscule electronic audience. The market for e-books slowly began to change with the development of portable readers, though true acceptance began only after the development of a new paperlike display technology, known as e-ink or e-paper, by the E Ink Corporation of Cambridge, Mass., based on prior research from the Massachusetts Institute of Technology's Media Laboratory. Sony introduced the first e-ink reader, the Librié, in 2004, and Amazon.com began marketing a similar portable e-ink reader, the Kindle, in 2007. Other e-book providers include iRex, a division of Royal Philips Electronics, and cell phone company China Mobile. Bookstore operator Barnes & Noble has an

Portable e-book readers like the Amazon Kindle, shown peeking out from among a row of books, have changed the landscape of book publishing and marketing. Bloomberg via Getty Images

e-bookstore on its Web site and offers e-books that can be read on several devices, including PCs, Apple's iPhone and Research in Motion's BlackBerry smartphones, and Barnes & Noble's own e-book reader, called NOOK.

The inclusion of DRM software in these devices has encouraged publishers to offer selected titles, especially current best sellers, as e-books. As sales of such portable readers have grown, demand for pirated e-books also has increased. Some critics of DRM assert that piracy actually increases sales. A study in 2009 by the consulting firm O'Reilly Media and the book publisher Random House seemed to support that assertion. The Canadian science-fiction author Cory Doctorow has long held this view, as he gives away electronic versions of all of his writings, which he asserts only increases sales of his books. On the other hand, American science-fiction author Harlan Ellison probably represented the views of most writers when he threatened, "If you put your hand in my pocket, you'll drag back six inches of bloody stump."

In addition, book publishers have worried that letting libraries offer e-books would make consumers less inclined to buy print versions, because downloading e-books made library use easier. As a result, some book publishers have refused to allow their e-books to be offered through libraries.

The Kindle produced the first consumer privacy issue associated with e-books when in 2009 Amazon, realizing that it lacked the rights to sell George Orwell's novels *1984* and *Animal Farm* online, refunded the 99-cent purchase price to customers and remotely deleted copies of the books already downloaded to nearly 2,000 Kindle customers. Amazon was slammed with a barrage of criticism, made more intense because *1984* details how powerful rulers can dominate peoples' lives. A Michigan high-school student whose copy of *1984* was deleted sued Amazon, and in September the case was settled out of court. Amazon agreed to pay $150,000 (to be donated to charity) and apologized for deleting the books. As part of the settlement, the company also pledged not to delete e-books from U.S. customers' Kindle units in the future unless the user agreed, the user wanted a refund or failed to make the electronic payment, a court ordered a book deleted, or removing a book was necessary to eliminate malicious software.

The Kindle case illuminated the difficulties of determining ownership in the digital age. Under the Kindle license agreement, e-books purchased by users were licensed, not owned, and the license also allowed Amazon to alter the e-book service. Attorneys indicated that it was unclear whether the license agreement allowed Amazon to delete e-book content that consumers had bought and downloaded to a Kindle.

CHAPTER 5

A WORLD OF CONTENT

The ensemble of hardware and software that makes up cyberspace can be seen as converging to bring all known information to the individual while, at the same time, making it possible for the individual to disseminate information at will into the reaches of cyberspace. The user is also a provider, the reader is also a writer. both roles meet in the act of learning and the creation of content.

MEDIA CONVERGENCE

Media convergence is a phenomenon involving the interlocking of computing and information technology companies, telecommunications networks, and content providers from the publishing worlds of newspapers, magazines, music, radio, television, films, and entertainment software. Media convergence brings together the "three Cs"—computing, communications, and content.

Convergence occurs at two primary levels:

1. Technologies—creative content has been converted into industry-standard digital forms for delivery through broadband or wireless networks for display on various computer or computer-like devices, from cellular telephones to tablet computers to digital video recorders (DVRs) hooked up to televisions.

2. Industries—companies across the business spectrum from media to telecommunications

to technology have merged or formed strategic alliances in order to develop new business models that can profit from the growing consumer expectation for "on-demand" content.

Some industry analysts see media convergence as marking the twilight of the "old media" of print and broadcasting

In addition to functioning as a cellular telephone, Apple's touch-screen iPhone, released in 2007, has a built-in Web browser for viewing Internet content over wireless telephone networks and WiFi connections. The iPhone also can be used as a multimedia playback device for listening to music or viewing videos.

and the rise of "new media" associated with digital publishing. Among the major changes associated with digital publishing is the growth of a "flatter" publishing structure that allows one-to-one and many-to-many distributions of content. This development contrasts sharply with the one-to-many distribution that was characteristic of 20th-century mass communications. Digital publishing also has empowered many ordinary individuals to become involved directly or through collaborative efforts in creating new content because of the dramatically reduced barriers to producing and distributing digital content over the Internet.

While these developments have challenged the business models of old media as they developed in the 20th century, the ability of these companies to adapt to the changing landscape should not be dismissed. Old media, or big media, is very experienced in producing content, attracting and aggregating audiences, and anticipating changes in consumer demands and expectations. Big media companies are also highly capitalized and often enter the new media environment through mergers, acquisitions, and strategic partnerships, as seen with NBC Universal, an American media conglomerate, which formed a partnership with the Microsoft Corporation to develop the MSNBC cable and Internet news service in 1996. Similarly, in 2005 international media entrepreneur Rupert Murdoch acquired MySpace, an Internet social networking Web site, in order to leverage his News Corporation into an established online community.

Convergence in Newspapers and Magazines

Virtually all major newspapers and magazines now operate a Web site. It has been an ongoing challenge for these publishing industries to assess the exact impact that an online component has on their business models and their broader operational structures as distributors of news, information, and entertainment.

In modern societies worldwide, consumers have come to expect access to the latest news from television broadcasts, such as those presented by the Cable News Network (CNN) and the British Broadcasting Corporation (BBC), instead of having to wait until the next day to read about it in the newspapers. In addition, various Web sites sprang up in the 1990s to specialize in classified advertisements—for everything from jobs to used items to lonely hearts—in direct competition with newspapers. In order to compete with the growth of television news networks and the Internet, newspapers began to move online in the 1990s. This created something of a feedback loop as consumers came to depend on the newspaper Web sites for current news, and the papers were thus induced to put more resources into competing on the Web; this in turn led to the addition of still more multimedia content, such as photographs, audio, and video, as well as blogs (essentially editorials) and forums to attract interaction with their readers. None of these moves was of much help, however, because of the loss of newsstand sales and advertising revenues for print copies. Indeed, some in the news industry have predicted that classified advertising eventually will disappear from all newspapers.

Thus far, the challenges have been less sharply delineated for magazines, although in both cases it is apparent that, even as geography and scale have diminished in significance as determinants of potential market size and profitability, it is those mastheads with high credibility among consumers (such as *The Wall Street Journal*, *The Guardian*, and *The Economist*) that have fared best in the convergent online media space.

Convergence in the Music Industry

The arrival of Napster in 1999 marked the emergence of decentralized peer-to-peer (P2P) sharing of music over the Internet. At its peak in 2001, there were as many as 1.5 million people simultaneously sharing files worldwide by using Napster's software, and Napster had embedded in the consciousness of consumers the idea of downloading

songs from the Internet—bypassing the purchase of established distribution forms, such as records, tapes, or compact discs (CDs).

Napster was shut down as a P2P network in 2001 after a successful court injunction was granted to the Recording Industry Association of America (RIAA), but the idea that songs could be downloaded, stored, and shared through networked personal computers had clearly caught on. New P2P illegal file-sharing Web sites popped up about as fast as the RIAA could shut them down, with the association often inadvertently charging children in its attempt to discourage digital sharing. Meanwhile, the music industry generally refused to see any merit in instituting its own digital distribution. It took a technology company, Apple Inc., to take advantage of this pent-up demand by launching an online Web site (the iTunes Store) in 2003 to sell songs, and later videos, for play on the company's iPod portable digital media player, using the company's iTunes music program. By 2006 Apple had sold more than 100 million iPods, and by 2010 10 billion songs had been downloaded from the iTunes Store, with all of the songs paid for and the royalties returned to record companies and artists.

Following Apple's lead, other commercial online music services were launched, such as those by Amazon.com and Microsoft. However, the largest record companies generally refused to participate or allowed only a small sample of their record catalogs to be sold online in digital form. One complaint by the music industry was Apple's flat pricing structure, in which all songs were sold for the same price. In 2008 Amazon.com negotiated a deal with most of the major record companies whereby their songs would be priced at different levels according to market considerations.

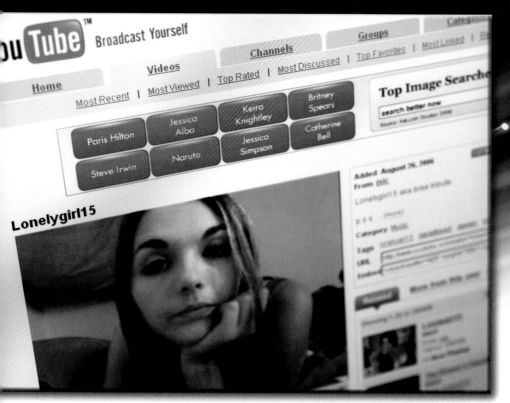

Media giant Viacom claimed in 2007 that some content posted on the popular video-sharing site YouTube violates copyright law. Bloomberg via Getty Images

Convergence in Radio, Television, and Movies

Podcasting, a neologism from a combination of *iPod* and *broadcasting*, refers to digital audiovisual files that are distributed over the Internet, typically to personal computers and portable media devices. Although podcasting existed before Apple introduced the iPod in 2001, few people listened to or viewed such files on portable devices before that time. Public broadcasters, such as the BBC and, in the United States, National Public Radio (NPR), were quick to act on the potential of podcasting in order to extend the audience reach of their radio programming, as it eliminated the time dependency of traditional broadcasting schedules. Soon television shows could be bought for a small fee and watched on iPods, cellular telephones, and other portable devices.

As access to broadband networks proliferated in the 2000s, the movie industry began experiencing concerns similar to what the music industry had dealt with in the 1990s. Although the film industry also had devoted considerable attention to preventing content from being copied and distributed by unauthorized individuals over the Internet, the great size of movie files, compared with songs, gave the industry more time to adjust to the notion of selling digital versions of their content through regular commercial outlets. In particular, the film and television industries have a longer history of dealing with the recording and renting of their content by the public. In addition, they have experimented with supplying user-requested, or on-demand, content through special broadband networks set up for the purpose.

Nevertheless, the scene was complicated by the arrival of YouTube in 2005, a Web site that allows individuals to share videos, some of which have infringed on copyrighted material. In response, in 2007 the American media conglomerate Viacom Inc., which includes various cable and satellite television networks as well as motion-picture studios among its holdings, filed a lawsuit against YouTube and its owners, the search engine company Google Inc. (which had acquired YouTube in 2006), for breach of copyright.

MARKET FRAGMENTATION IN THE INTERNET AGE

Traditionally, advertisers could rely on reaching a large, stable audience of potential customers through print, radio, and television ads. While such traditional advertising media helped to establish some of the most successful and well-known brands, audience fragmentation in the 21st century complicated the picture, with the nature of different digital content delivery devices, such as cellular telephones and PDAs, often having a dramatic impact on the length of time that any particular message could hold the consumer's attention. While consumers could usually be relied on to wait through 30-second radio and television ads, few people demonstrated that much patience for similar ads on their mobile digital devices or their personal computers.

More recently, media distribution models have been challenged by the concept of the "long tail," or the idea that there are actually more total consumers for niche material than there are for the "best sellers." This marketing phenomenon is demonstrated by the experience of the online bookseller Amazon.com, which collectively sells far more books from the "poor sales" category than it does from the best-seller lists. As the company expanded from sales and delivery of tangible, material goods into electronic delivery of digitized books, music, and films, the long-tail phenomenon continued to be apparent. In the case of such online merchants, the distribution of digital media content has revealed both a greater heterogeneity of consumer preferences than was traditionally assumed and the value of business models associated with making more diverse content available to the consumer. A long-predicted similar broadening of consumer offerings began at the end of the 20th century in television, where the availability of cable and satellite for distributing new television channels greatly expanded the drive to exploit every available niche market, be it for strongman competitions or for poetry readings. A particularly interesting development, sometimes referred to as the golden convergence, has been the battle to control the home-entertainment space in the 21st century. The start of this convergence can be seen in the creation of television channels dedicated to electronic gaming from one side and the inclusion of Internet and television recording and playback features in video game machines from the other side.

Still another growing battle in the age of the Internet has concerned the sharing of revenue, not just between the technology, communications, and content companies but with all of the people involved in creating and producing the content. Agents for the actors, writers, costume and set designers, and sundry guild members associated with any major production have expressed regrets that they failed to fight for a more equitable distribution of the proceeds from the sale of discs containing their clients' works. The trend to distribution of such works through the Internet is now clearer, however. Typically, contracts for the various artistic crafts have not included any form of revenue sharing for the new digital distribution channels. With so much money at stake, all sides have been reluctant to compromise, which has led to bitter confrontations and strikes.

WEB 2.0: ONLINE COMMUNITIES AND SOCIAL NETWORKING

The global popularization of the Internet was accompanied by a boom in electronic commerce, or e-commerce. British computer scientist Tim Berners-Lee, creator of the World Wide Web, soon argued that this focus on commerce was misplaced, as it assumed that Internet users remained primarily consumers of information and content developed by others for online distribution. He argued that the core design principle of the Internet instead lay in the scope that it offered people to interact with one another, including in collaborations in which they became content creators in their own right.

The concept of collaborative participation by the general public in the generation of content, a concept that has come to be called Web 2.0, is centrally important to understanding new media in the 21st century. Web 2.0 applications have features that enable communications in a flat structure—rather than through a centralized hierarchy—which has been shown to facilitate user participation, interactivity, collaborative learning, and social networking. Web 2.0 applications also generate positive networking effects from harnessing collective intelligence, so that the quality of participation increases as the numbers participating increase, which in turn attracts more users to the Web sites. On the other hand, growth is sometimes accompanied by the arrival of malicious individuals seeking to disrupt or sabotage such social projects.

Some leading Web 2.0 sites include Flickr (photography), Wikipedia (online encyclopaedia), YouTube (videos), various aggregated blog Web sites (Blogger, LiveJournal, and Technorati), and "personal profile" Web sites (MySpace, Facebook, and Friendster). In general, all of these Web sites share certain guiding principles. They are designed with minimal centralized controls, with the focus on users and their interactions with one another. Whenever possible, they employ open-source software that can be adapted and modified according to changing requirements. Relatively simple and "lightweight" in their design, they have minimal administrative, start-up, and ongoing development costs.

Online communities attained more prominence in the 1990s as it became apparent that computer-mediated communication had acquired the capacity to enable new forms of community building and participation both in public life and in virtual reality worlds. In the case of the latter, participants sometimes argued that their virtual lives were more interesting and fulfilling than their real lives. While online communities generated new forms of social networking for some—and also raised a range of new issues around the ethics of online communication—by the early 2000s it was apparent that there was a growing bifurcation between these communities and the rest of the Web, where information and content are abundant but the scope for users to interact with Web sites and one another remains highly circumscribed.

Yochai Benkler, an American legal scholar specializing in Internet law, argues in *The Wealth of Networks* (2006) that the Internet provides a necessary but not sufficient condition for the rise of what he calls social production. According to Benkler, three further necessary conditions are:

> *First, nonproprietary strategies....As the material barrier...is removed, these basic nonmarket, nonproprietary, motivations and organizational forms should in principle become even more important to the information production system. Second...the rise of nonmarket production.... The fact that every such effort is available to anyone connected to the network, from anywhere, has led to the emergence of coordinate effects, where the aggregate effect of individual action, even when it is not self-consciously cooperative, produces the coordinate effect of a new and rich information environment. Third, and likely most radical...is the rise of effective, large-scale cooperative efforts—peer production of information, knowledge, and culture. These are typified by the emergence of free and open-source software.*

COPYRIGHT AND DIGITAL RIGHTS MANAGEMENT

Copyright law is derived from the principle that neither the creator nor the general public should be able to appropriate all the benefits that flow from the creation of a new, original work. It presumes that original forms of creative expression can belong to individuals, who have both a moral right to ownership and a legal economic right to derive material benefit from the use of their ideas and works by others. On the other hand, copyright laws also recognize that original ideas and works are drawn from and inspired by a preexisting pool of knowledge and works. Thus, there is a need to guarantee that new ideas and works also make their way into the public domain for fair use by others in order to ensure further progress. In order to balance competing claims, copyright law gives control over some rights to the creators and distributors of content and control over other rights to the general public.

The digitalization of content has challenged traditional copyright laws on two fronts. First, it has enabled nearly cost-free reproduction and large-scale distribution of digital content. Second, existing digital content easily can be remixed and "mashed-up" (combined in various ways) with other content to produce new works. In response to these changes, copyright holders have sought greater protection through legal and technological remedies. The various technological schemes are collectively known as digital rights management (DRM), which include different mechanisms to prevent digital files from being copied or shared over networks. As many critics have observed, DRM schemes are technically complex to apply, often generate interoperability problems between devices, and diminish consumer privacy by requiring complex registration systems. In addition, DRM generates new imbalances between the controllers and users of copyrighted materials, as fair use cannot be embedded in such mechanisms.

As an alternative to DRM or further tightening of copyright laws and litigation between copyright owners and users, in 2001 Lawrence Lessig, founder of the Center for Internet and Society at Stanford Law School in California, founded Creative Commons, a nonprofit organization dedicated to making copyright material more accessible and its terms of access more negotiable in the digital environment. A key aim of Creative Commons was to simplify for creative people across the artistic, educational, scientific, and digital production domains the process of designating in advance, and independently of those who distribute their content as commercial products, how others can use or modify their works. There are four types of Creative Commons licenses: (1) use with attribution; (2) use for noncommercial purposes only; (3) use only of the original work, with no derivative works; and (4) use on a "share alike" basis (the license for the new work shares the same conditions of use as that from which it was derived). These licenses aim to overcome bottlenecks presented by current copyright and intellectual arrangements, such as the locating of initial content creators, the existence of different levels of rights in different domains and for different forms of use, and the restrictions on the abilities of users to negotiate directly with the original creators of copyrighted material.

BLOGGING AND ONLINE REPORTING

Blogging is the practice of creating and maintaining a blog (that is, a Web log or Weblog), an online journal where an individual, group, or corporation presents a record of activities, thoughts, or beliefs. Some blogs operate mainly as news filters, collecting various online sources and adding short comments and Internet links. Other blogs concentrate on presenting original material. In addition, many blogs provide a forum to allow visitors to leave comments and interact with the publisher. "To blog" is the act of composing material for a blog. Materials are largely written, but pictures, audio, and videos are important elements of many blogs. The "blogosphere" is the online universe of blogs.

From Geeks to Mainstream

The World Wide Web and the idea of a blog appeared at the same time. Tim Berners-Lee, often described as the Web's inventor, created the first "blog" in 1992 to outline and render visible the ongoing development of the Web and the software necessary to navigate this new space. Web history, especially the early growth of Web servers and sites, is chronicled on the various "What's New" pages in the archives of the National Center for Supercomputing Applications (NCSA) at the University of Illinois at Urbana-Champaign. Another example of a blog that existed before the word was coined is Slashdot. Following its debut in September 1997, Slashdot operated as a clearinghouse for information in its "News for Nerds," with a small set of editors who decided what to publish of numerous articles and news items submitted by the "geek" community. Indeed, Web sites mentioned on Slashdot were often overwhelmed, leading to a condition now known as being "slashdotted."

In December 1997, Jorn Barger, an early online presence, coined the term *web log* to describe his Web site RobotWisdom.com. In early 1999 another individual with considerable online experience, Peter Merholz, began to employ the term *blog* on his site Peterme.com. While the history of the term is pretty well settled, the same cannot be said of the identity of the first blogger. Depending on the definition of a blog, Berners-Lee may not qualify as the first blogger. Claimants to this title include Justin Hall, a college student who started an online list at links.net in 1994; Carolyn Burke, who began publishing Carolyn's Diary online in 1995; and Dave Winer, who has published Scripting News online since April 1, 1997.

The growth of the blogosphere from there was nothing short of remarkable. Technorati, Inc., a Web site and organization dedicated to mapping and searching the blogosphere, reported that by October 2005 there were 19.6 million blogs, a number that continued to grow to the point that in 2008 Technorati was able to report that it

A 2006 screenshot of Iranian President Mahmoud Ahmadinejad's blog. Blogs can advance a political agenda, serve as a marketing tool, or simply allow individuals to express themselves to a wide audience. AFP/Getty Images

had indexed some 133 million blogs since 2002. By then, however, such numbers had started to lose their meaning. On the one hand, the number of active blogs (that is, blogs that regularly received posts) was considerably smaller (fewer than one million blogs were posted every day); on the other hand, the considerable amount of blogging done within social networking sites such as MySpace, as well as the microblogging done on services such as Twitter, were not counted as blogs. So the blogosphere was either larger or smaller than Technorati's estimation, depending on how one viewed blogging. Nevertheless, by any method of counting blogs or by any definition of blogging, the blogosphere has arrived very quickly at a position of importance in the lives of millions of people. Also of importance is the growth of blogs in languages other than English, especially Chinese.

Despite the overwhelming number of blogs, very few individuals make a living as a blogger. A few individuals earn money from their Web sites by carrying ads and appeals for funds, and some blogs are financed by corporate or organizational owners; nevertheless, most bloggers derive nonmonetary rewards from their activity. In particular, blogs offer ordinary individuals the ultimate soapbox and an opportunity to create their own digital identity or personal brand.

One reason for the proliferation of blogs is the ease with which they can be established and maintained. Many services and software systems are available that allow an individual to set up a blog in less than an hour. Of course, updating a blog is essential for maintaining its presence and importance. Statistics on blogs that are started but not updated remain elusive, but the proportion is undoubtedly substantial.

Like the fad for personal Web pages in the 1990s, the proliferation of blogs has led to the creation of Web sites that group blogs, often with a similar political emphasis or subject orientation, to form "superblogs." An example of this phenomenon is The Huffington Post, founded in 2005 by American author and syndicated newspaper columnist Arianna Huffington, which hosts dozens of other bloggers who post mostly on politics and current affairs.

DIALOGUE

In addition to the frequency of updates, the thing that distinguishes most blogs from ordinary Web pages is the inclusion of forums for readers to post comments to which the blogger might respond. The degree to which dissenting views are tolerated depends on the publisher, but most Web sites must regularly prune "spam"—insertions of commercial and pornographic ads into the text of an apparent comment or the use of insulting and defamatory language. Trackback, an Internet function, facilitates communication by allowing bloggers to monitor who is reading and discussing their site. In turn, bloggers often post a "blogroll," or a list of other blogs that they read and respect. Blogging is a conversational activity that seeks to create a community or reflect an existing community.

For a corporation, blogs can be used to advertise corporate products and practices and for two-way communication with consumers. For nonprofit entities such as charities, blogs allow officials to discuss their goals and actions in pursuit of a common end.

A growing phenomenon involves people who start blogs, often anonymously, to disparage someone or something that they dare not attack openly—such as their company, boss, school, or teacher—or to tilt at some organization that "done 'em wrong." In several instances, individuals have lost their jobs when employers discovered their blogs.

CITIZEN JOURNALISM

A phenomenon related to blogging is so-called citizen journalism, which has expanded its worldwide influence in spite of continuing concerns over whether "citizen" journalists are "real" journalists. Citizens in disaster zones have provided instant text and visual reporting from the scene. People in countries affected by violence have used a variety of technological tools to share information about hot spots. Swirling in the background of these developments is a debate over whether the term *citizen journalism* is itself accurate.

The term *citizen journalism* is derived from South Korean online entrepreneur Oh Yeon Ho's declaration in 2000 that "every citizen is a reporter." Oh and three South Korean colleagues started an online daily newspaper in 2000 because, he said, they were dissatisfied with the traditional South Korean press. Unable to afford the costs of hiring professionals and printing a newspaper, they started OhmyNews, a Web site that used volunteers to generate its content. In a speech on the site's seventh anniversary, Oh, the firm's president and CEO, noted that the news site began with 727 citizen reporters and had grown to 50,000 contributors reporting from 100 countries by 2007.

Since OhmyNews's adoption of "Every citizen is a reporter" as its motto, the Internet has spawned thousands of news sites and millions of bloggers. Traditional news organizations, while battling declining readership and viewership, have leaped into the fray with their own Web sites and blogs by their own journalists, and many newspapers have invited readers to contribute community news to the papers' Web sites. Citizens have started their own "hyperlocal" online news sites to cover happenings in their neighbourhoods or specialized topics of interest that are not reported by larger media organizations.

Among those who study and nurture citizen journalism, the term often goes by other names. In a 2007 article for Online Journalism Review, J.D. Lasica called it "participatory journalism," though he described it as "a slippery creature. Everyone knows what audience participation means, but when does that translate into journalism? Alas, there's no simple answer." Dan Gillmor, founder and director of the Center for Citizen Media—a nonprofit affiliated jointly with the Walter Cronkite School of Journalism and Mass Communication at Arizona State University and the Berkman Center for Internet & Society at Harvard University Law School—and author of the book *We the Media: Grassroots Journalism by the People, for the People* (2004), also rejects any single definition for the transformation in news that began taking place in the late 1990s. "It's a time of incredible exploration," because of the democratization of access to inexpensive and ubiquitous publishing tools, says Gillmor. New York University journalism professor and online media thinker Jay Rosen came close to a unified theory of citizen journalism in a July 14, 2008, post on his PressThink blog: "When the people formerly known as the audience employ the press tools they have in their possession to inform one another, *that's* citizen journalism."

People around the world have participated in this phenomenon. Earthquake victims in China's Sichuan province in May 2008 took up cell phones to send text messages and images from the disaster zone to the world. When the Kenyan government shut down traditional media outlets in the violent aftermath of disputed national elections in late 2007, Africa-based bloggers encouraged citizens to use their cell phones to report incidents of violence by voice, text messages, and images. Citizens by the thousands did exactly that. Within the first two weeks of 2008, some of those bloggers created www.Ushahidi.com, which combined Google maps and a "crowdsourced" database of violent incidents to give readers a near real-time visual glimpse of where outbreaks were occurring. In late November 2008 some bystanders used social networking Web sites such as Twitter and Flickr to upload live reports, digital photos, and video of the terrorist attacks in Mumbai (Bombay), while others used their cell phones to send updated reports to more traditional news services or to transmit text messages to people trapped inside the hotels under attack. This pattern has been repeated—and intensified—during subsequent disasters, from the Haiti earthquake of 2010 to the earthquake and tsunami that struck Japan in 2011.

An experiment in "hybrid" citizen journalism at the HuffingtonPost, an American news and commentary Web site, generated controversy during the 2008 U.S. presidential primary campaign when Mayhill Fowler, an amateur writer and supporter of candidate Barack Obama, reported that the Democrat had described working-class Pennsylvanians as "bitter." The incident, buried in a longer post on the site's OffTheBus blog, gave Republicans and some of Obama's Democratic rivals ammunition to call him an "elitist." Fowler's report drew criticism from other media. Some attacked as unethical her reporting of remarks made at a private fund-raiser that had excluded traditional journalists. Rosen, cocreator with Arianna Huffington of the blog, defended Fowler. Rosen wrote in a post on PressThink that he and Huffington "felt that participants in political life had a right to report on what they saw and heard themselves, not as journalists claiming no attachments but as citizens *with* attachments who were relinquishing none of their rights." Traditional journalists disagreed vehemently with Rosen's position, citing the long-held ethical belief that journalists should remain

This image grab from an amateur video shows a protester defacing the image of Pres. Bashar al-Assad during the 2011 political uprising in Syria. AFP/ Getty Images

independent from those whom they cover. Most traditional news organizations, in fact, prohibited political involvement by their reporters.

Jan Schaffer, executive director of J-Lab: The Institute for Interactive Journalism, prefers the term "citizen media makers instead of citizen journalists because we need to understand that the kinds of things we're seeing have their own value propositions, and those may be very different from the values we associate with conventional journalism. Most citmedia makers don't aspire to be 'journalists' and I think we need to be careful not to require them to be members of a tribe that they don't necessarily want to belong to."

J-Lab, based in Washington, D.C., provides start-up funds to citizen media projects through an incubator program called New Voices. Projects that have received funds include a proposal by Kent (Ohio) State University to train student journalists and general aviation enthusiasts to write about Ohio's 166 public airports, 772 private airfields, and 18,000 pilots for online publication and for newspapers, public radio, and television. Another New Voices-funded project started a digital neighbourhood newspaper using citizen reporters and aiming to build a sense of community across racial, ethnic, and income divisions in Lexington, Ky.

Schaffer cites many examples of the variety of citizen-journalism efforts: networked sites, such as NowPublic.com and Helium.com, that have sought to aggregate citizen photos, video footage, and articles from around the world; conventional media that have attracted citizen-generated content, including CNN's iReport.com and the Denver-based YourHub.com; microlocal community news sites such as NewCastleNow.org and ForumHome.org that have been founded by ordinary citizens to fill an information vacuum; and microlocal sites founded by former journalists, such as Baristanet.com, MinnPost.com, NewHavenIndependent.com, and HuffingtonPost.com. Bloggers in Third World countries have often filled in when media were government-controlled or absent with sites such as GlobalVoicesOnline.org, or they used cell phone text messages to report on crisis hotspots. For its efforts, Ushahidi.com won one of J-Lab's 2008 Knight-Batten Awards for Innovations in Journalism. In Schaffer's words, citizen media "is not just one big phenomenon, but the onset of many different niches being occupied by various citizen media makers."

DISTANCE LEARNING

Distance learning—also called distance education, e-learning, and online learning—is a form of education in which the main elements include physical separation

WIKILEAKS

A media organization and Web site that functions as a clearinghouse for classified or otherwise privileged information, WikiLeaks was founded in 2006 by Australian computer programmer and activist Julian Assange. Assange was inspired to create WikiLeaks by Daniel Ellsberg's 1971 release of the Pentagon Papers, a classified government history of the U.S. role in Indochina from World War II until 1968. Observing that two years had elapsed between Ellsberg's obtaining the Pentagon Papers and their publication in *The New York Times*, Assange sought to streamline the whistle-blowing process. In 2006 he created the basic design for the site on a computer in Australia, but wikileaks.org soon moved to servers in Sweden (later adding redundant systems in other countries) because of that country's robust press-protection laws. Although WikiLeaks relied on volunteer labour for much of its daily operation, it deviated from the traditional "wiki" formula in that its content was not editable by end users.

WikiLeaks received its first batch of sensitive documents not from a whistle-blower but from The Onion Router (Tor), an encryption network designed to allow users to transmit data anonymously. A WikiLeaks volunteer mined the data emerging from Tor, eventually collecting more than a million documents and providing the site with its first scoop—a message from a Somali rebel leader encouraging the use of hired gunmen to assassinate government officials. Posted to the site in December 2006, the document's authenticity was never verified, but the story of WikiLeaks and questions regarding the ethics of its methods soon overshadowed it.

In November 2007 the site posted the standard operating procedures for the U.S. military's detention facility at Guantánamo Bay, Cuba. The following year the wikileaks.org site was briefly shut down as a result of legal action in the United States, but mirrors of the site, registered in Belgium (wikileaks.be), Germany (wikileaks.de), and the Christmas Islands (wikileaks.cx), were unaffected.

In 2009 the site made news when it released a cache of internal e-mails from East Anglia University's Climatic Research Unit. Global warming skeptics seized on them as proof of a conspiracy to silence debate on the subject or conceal data. A subsequent series of investigations found shortcomings in the peer review process but cleared the scientists of intentional wrongdoing.

In 2010 WikiLeaks posted a flurry of documents—almost half a million in total—relating to the U.S. wars in Iraq and Afghanistan. While much of the information was already in the public domain, the administration of Pres. Barack Obama criticized the leaks as a threat to U.S. national security. The site also made public an edited video, filmed in 2007 from the gun camera of a U.S. attack helicopter, that depicted the killing of a dozen people, including two Reuters employees. In November 2010 WikiLeaks released some 250,000 classified diplomatic cables between the U.S. State Department and its embassies and consulates around the world. Those documents dated mostly from 2007 to 2010 but included some dating back as far as 1966. Among the wide-ranging topics covered in those secret documents were behind-the-scenes U.S. efforts to politically and economically isolate Iran, primarily in response to fears of Iran's development of nuclear weapons.

WikiLeaks began publishing another round of secret files from the Guantánamo Bay facility in April 2011. The documents contained detailed information about the majority of prisoners detained at Guantánamo from 2002 to 2008, including photographs, health records, and assessments of the potential threat posed by each prisoner. The files also indicated that dozens of detainees had passed through radicalized British mosques prior to their departure for Afghanistan and, ultimately, their capture by U.S. forces.

of teachers and students during instruction and the use of various technologies to facilitate student-teacher and student-student communication. Distance learning traditionally has focused on nontraditional students, such as full-time workers, military personnel, and nonresidents or individuals in remote regions who are unable to attend classroom lectures. However, distance learning is now becoming an established part of the educational world. In U.S. higher education alone, more than 5.6 million university students were enrolled in at least one online course in the autumn of 2009, up from 1.6 million in 2002. More than half of all two-year and four-year degree-granting institutions of higher education in the United States offer distance education courses, primarily through the

Elementary school students in Aledo, Texas, are instructed by a staffer at the Botanical Research Institute of Texas, based miles away in Fort Worth. Fort Worth Star-Telegram/McClatchy-Tribune/Getty Images

Internet, about one-quarter of American students take at least one online course each term. Higher education experts predict that the demand for online course work will only continue to grow.

An increasing number of colleges provide distance-learning opportunities. A pioneer in the field is the University of Phoenix, which was founded in Arizona in 1976 and is now the largest private school in the world, with more than 400,000 enrolled students. It is one of the earliest adopters of distance learning technology, although more than half of its students spend some time in classrooms on one of its dozens of campuses in the United States, Canada, and Puerto Rico. A precise figure for the international enrollment in distance learning is unavailable, but the enrollment at two of the largest public universities that heavily utilize distance learning methods gives some indication: in the early 21st century the Indira Gandhi National Open University, headquartered in New Delhi, India, had an enrollment in excess of 1.5 million students, and the China Central Radio and TV University, headquartered in Beijing, had more than 500,000 students.

Many U.S. states have committed resources to the facilitation of distance learning. For example, Iowa has built an extensive fibre-optic network, called the Iowa Communications Network (ICN), to connect more than 700 classrooms at every level, from kindergarten through university. The ICN facilitates live video for instruction, allows for extensive Internet-based courses, and serves as a high-speed link to the Web. Similarly, South Dakota has created the Digital Dakota Network (DDN), which connects more than 400 schools and colleges and enables the delivery of thousands of courses and events each year. Network Nebraska has been established to serve distance learning in the state's schools, colleges, and universities.

Students and institutions embrace distance education with good reason. Universities benefit by adding students without having to construct classrooms and housing, and students reap the advantages of being able to work where and when they choose. Public-school systems offer specialty courses such as small-enrollment languages and Advanced Placement classes without having to set up multiple classrooms. In addition, home-schooled children gain access to centralized instruction.

CHARACTERISTICS OF DISTANCE LEARNING

Various terms have been used to describe the phenomenon of distance learning. Strictly speaking, distance learning (the student's activity) and distance teaching (the teacher's activity) together make up distance education.

Common variations include e-learning or online learning, used when the Internet is the medium; virtual learning, which usually refers to courses taken outside a classroom by primary- or secondary-school pupils (and also typically using the Internet); correspondence education, the long-standing method in which individual instruction is conducted by mail; and open learning, the system common in Europe for learning through the "open" university.

Four characteristics distinguish distance education. First, distance education is by definition carried out through institutions; it is not self-study or a nonacademic learning environment. The institutions may or may not offer traditional classroom-based instruction as well, but they are eligible for accreditation by the same agencies as those employing traditional methods.

Second, geographic separation is inherent in distance learning, and time may also separate students and teachers. Accessibility and convenience are important advantages of this mode of education. Well-designed programs can also bridge intellectual, cultural, and social differences between students.

Third, interactive telecommunications connect the learning group with each other and with the teacher. Most often, electronic communications, such as e-mail, are used, but traditional forms of communication, such as the postal system, may also play a role. Whatever the medium, interaction is essential to distance education, as it is to any education. The connections of learners, teachers, and instructional resources become less dependent on physical proximity as communications systems become more sophisticated and widely available; consequently, the Internet, cell phones, and e-mail have contributed to the rapid growth in distance education.

Finally, distance education, like any education, establishes a learning group, sometimes called a learning community, which is composed of students, a teacher, and instructional resources—i.e., the books, sound, video, and graphic displays that allow the student to access the content of instruction. Social networking on the Internet promotes the idea of community building. On sites such as MySpace, Facebook, and YouTube, users construct profiles, identify members ("friends") with whom they share a connection, and build new communities of like-minded persons. In the distance-education setting, such networking can enable students' connections with each other and thereby reduce their sense of isolation.

The most commonly expressed concern about distance learning and teaching was whether the process was as effective as traditional education. Research into the question produced clear results: if all factors were taken into account, the learning outcomes were equivalent. Factors such as course organization, teacher involvement, class interaction, and feedback were critical to the effectiveness of instruction, whether in a classroom or at a distance.

WEB-BASED COURSES AND SERVICES

Although the theoretical trend in distance learning beginning in the 1990s seemed to be toward a stronger reliance on video, sound, and other multimedia, in practice most successful programs have predominately utilized electronic texts and simple text-based communications. The reasons for this are partly practical—individual instructors often bear the burden of producing their own multimedia—but also reflect an evolving understanding of the central benefits of distance learning. It is now seen as a way of facilitating communication between teachers and students, as well as among students, by removing the time constraints associated with sharing information in traditional classrooms or during instructors' office hours. Similarly, self-paced software educational systems, though still used for certain narrow types of training, have limited flexibility in responding and adapting to individual students, who typically demand some interaction with other humans in formal educational settings.

Modern distance learning courses employ Web-based course-management systems that incorporate digital reading materials, podcasts (recorded sessions for electronic listening or viewing at the student's leisure), e-mail, threaded (linked) discussion forums, chat rooms, and test-taking functionality in virtual (computer-simulated) classrooms. Both proprietary and open-source systems are common. Although most systems are generally asynchronous, allowing students access to most features whenever they wish, synchronous technologies, involving live video, sound, and shared access to electronic documents at scheduled times, are also used. Shared social spaces in the form of blogs, wikis (Web sites that can be modified by all classroom participants), and collaboratively edited documents are also used in educational settings, but to a lesser degree than similar spaces available on the Internet for socializing.

Alongside the growth in modern institutional distance learning has come Web-based or facilitated personal educational services, including e-tutoring, e-mentoring, and research assistance. Other services provide customized or generic school papers to students unable or unwilling to write their own. In addition, there are many educational assistance companies that help parents choose and contact local tutors for their children while the companies handle the contracts. The use of distance learning programs and tutoring services has increased particularly among parents who homeschool their children. Many universities have some online tutoring services for remedial help with reading, writing, and basic mathematics, and some even have online mentoring programs to help doctoral candidates through the dissertation process. Finally, many Web-based personal-assistant companies offer a range of services for adults seeking continuing education or professional development.

Open Universities

One of the most prominent types of educational institutions that makes use of distance learning is the open university, which is open in the sense that it admits nearly any adult. Since the mid-20th century the open university movement has gained momentum around the world, reflecting a desire for greater access to higher education by various constituencies, including nontraditional students, such as the disabled, military personnel, and prison inmates.

The origin of the movement can be traced to the University of London, which began offering degrees to external students in 1836. This paved the way for the growth of private correspondence colleges that prepared students for the University of London's examinations and enabled them to study independently for a degree without formally enrolling in the university. In 1946 the University of South Africa, headquartered in Pretoria, began offering correspondence courses, and in 1951 it was reconstituted to provide degree courses for external students only. A proposal in Britain for a "University of the Air" gained support in the early 1960s, leading to the founding of the Open University in 1971 in the recently formed town of Milton Keynes. By the end of the 1970s the university had 25,000 students, and it has since grown to annual enrollments in the hundreds of thousands. Open universities have spread across the world and are characterized as "mega-universities" because their enrollments may exceed hundreds of thousands, or even millions, of students in countries such as India, China, and Israel.

As one of the most successful nontraditional institutions with a research component, the Open University is a major contributor to both the administrative and pedagogical literature in the field of open universities. The university relies heavily on prepared materials and a tutor system. The printed text was originally the principal teaching medium in most Open University courses, but this changed somewhat with the advent of the Internet and computers, which enabled written assignments and materials to be distributed through the Web. For each course, the student is assigned a local tutor, who normally makes contact by telephone, mail, or e-mail to help with queries related to the academic materials. Students may also attend local face-to-face classes run by their tutor, and they may choose to form self-help groups with other students. Tutor-graded assignments and discussion sessions are the core aspects of this educational model. The tutors and interactions among individual students are meant to compensate for the lack of face-to-face lectures in the Open University. To emphasize the tutorial and individualized-learning aspects of its method, the Open University prefers to describe it as "supported open learning" rather than distance learning.

ACADEMIC ISSUES AND FUTURE DIRECTIONS

From the start, correspondence courses acquired a poor academic reputation, especially those provided by for-profit entities. As early as 1926, as a study commissioned by the Carnegie Corporation found, there was widespread fraud among correspondence schools in the United States, and there were no adequate standards to protect the public.

While the situation was later improved by the introduction of accrediting agencies that set standards for the delivery of distance learning programs, there has always been concern about the quality of the learning experience and the verification of student work. Additionally, the introduction of distance learning in traditional institutions raised fears that technology will someday completely eliminate real classrooms and human professors.

Because many distance learning programs are offered by for-profit institutions, distance learning has become associated with the commercialization of higher education. Generally, critics of this trend point to the potential exploitation of students who do not qualify for admission to traditional colleges and universities, the temptation in for-profit schools to lower academic standards in order to increase revenue, and a corporate administrative approach that emphasizes "market models" in educational curricula, or the designing of courses and curricula to appeal to a larger demographic in order to generate more institutional revenue—all of which point to a lowering of academic standards.

Distance learning, whether at for-profit or traditional universities, utilizes two basic economic models designed to reduce labour costs. The first model involves the substitution of labour with capital, while the second is based on the replacement of faculty with cheaper labour. Proponents of the first model have argued that distance learning offers economies of scale by reducing personnel costs after an initial capital investment for such things as Web servers, electronic texts and multimedia supplements, and Internet programs for interacting with students. However, many institutions that have implemented distance learning programs through traditional faculty and administrative structures have found that ongoing expenses associated with the programs may actually make them more expensive for the institution than traditional courses. The second basic approach, a labour-for-labour model, is to divide the faculty role into the functions of preparation, presentation, and assessment and to assign some of the functions to less-expensive workers. Open universities typically do this by forming committees to design courses and hiring part-time tutors to help struggling students and to grade papers, leaving the actual classroom instruction duties, if any, to the professors.

These distance learning models suggest that the largest change in education will come in altered roles for faculty and vastly different student experiences. Nevertheless, elite institutions, with small enrollments and well-endowed trust funds, seem likely to remain mostly unaffected, with the greatest transformations occurring in public institutions that have open-access missions and restricted funding.

CONCLUSION

The "network of networks" that is the Internet has grown phenomenally since its rather stealthy appearance in the late 1970s. As access to the Internet continues to shift to mobile personal devices, the precise direction of its continued growth in the decades to come will be harder to predict. The one certainty is that its growth will continue to open new worlds of opportunity and creativity—accompanied by new reasons for concern, vigilance, and even conflict. For better and worse, in an increasingly tech-savvy world, the Internet will be the place to go for a well-rounded understanding of life in the 21st century.

GLOSSARY

algorithm A step-by-step procedure for solving a problem or accomplishing some end, especially by a computer.

blog A Web site that contains an online personal journal with reflections, comments, and often hyperlinks provided by the writer.

botnet A network of compromised computers that can be controlled remotely and used to send out spam or perform other illicit functions.

broadband Of, relating to, or being a high-speed communications network.

data mining The process of discovering interesting and useful patterns and relationships in large volumes of data.

encryption The process of disguising information as "ciphertext," or data unintelligible to an unauthorized person.

Ethernet A computer network architecture consisting of various specified local-area network protocols, devices, and connection methods.

flash mob A group of strangers mobilized via Web sites, chat rooms, or text messages to take part in group activities in public places.

geotag Data added to media such as photographs that specifies the precise geographic location of the image.

hack To gain access to a computer illegally.

integrated circuit A tiny complex of electronic components and their connections that is produced in or on a small slice of material, such as silicon.

mainframe A digital computer designed for high-speed data processing via large-capacity disks and printers.

malware Malicious software designed to interfere with a computer's normal functioning, often transmitted through e-mail, Web sites, or attached hardware.

network A system of computers, peripherals, terminals, and databases connected by communications lines.

newsgroup An electronic bulletin board on the Internet devoted to a particular topic.

open source The practice of sharing computer programming source code and other information.

peer-to-peer (P2P) A type of computer network in which each computer acts as both a server and a client—supplying and receiving files—with bandwidth and processing distributed among all members of the network.

personal computer (PC) A general-purpose computer equipped with a microprocessor and designed to run especially commercial software for an individual user.

phishing A scam by which an e-mail user is duped into revealing personal or confidential information, which the scammer can use illicitly.

semiconductor Any of a class of crystalline solids that is intermediate in electrical conductivity between a conductor and an insulator.

social network An online community of individuals who exchange messages, share information, and, in some cases, cooperate on joint activities.

source code A computer program in its original programming language before translation into object code.

spam Unsolicited, usually commercial e-mail sent to a large number of addresses.

virus A portion of a program code that has been designed to secretly copy itself into other codes or computer files.

worm An independent computer program that is self-replicating, designed to erase or otherwise damage a computer's data or code.

zombie A computer connected to the Internet that allows a remote malware user to perform any action that the computer owner could on the infected computer.

BIBLIOGRAPHY

SILICON VALLEY AND THE INTERNET

Stuart W. Leslie, *The Cold War and American Science: The Military-Industrial-Academic Complex at MIT and Stanford* (1993), is a critical history of the growth of government-funded academic research, including early programs at MIT and Stanford from World War II. AnnaLee Saxenian, *Regional Advantage: Culture and Competition in Silicon Valley and Route 128* (1994), compares and contrasts the growth of high-technology companies around Stanford and MIT. C. Stewart Gillmor, *Fred Terman at Stanford: Building a Discipline, a University, and Silicon Valley* (2004), is a fine biography of Silicon Valley's founder.

An early history of the Internet is Janet Abbate, *Inventing the Internet* (1999). John Markoff, *What the Dormouse Said: How the Sixties Counterculture Shaped the Personal Computer Industry* (2005), is the only book to explicitly address the role of people such as Stewart Brand in the making of the personal computer.

Lawrence Lessig, *Code: Version 2.0* (2006), is an erudite discussion of how to properly regulate the Internet. Ronald Deibert et al. (eds.), *Access Denied: The Practice and Policy of Global Internet Filtering* (2008); and Jonathan Zittrain, *The Future of the Internet and How to Stop It* (2008), examine various efforts and potential threats to censor the Internet. Tim Berners-Lee and Mark Fischetti, *Weaving the Web: The Original Design and Ultimate Destiny of the World Wide Web by Its Inventor* (1999), argues that the

Web needs more scope for group creativity and less focus on electronic commerce.

Vinton G. Cerf and Robert E. Kahn, "A Protocol for Packet Network Intercommunication," *IEEE Transactions on Communications*, 22(5):637–648 (May 1974), is the paper that first detailed the overall architecture of the Internet and its operation. Barry M. Leiner et al., "The Past and Future History of the Internet," *Communications of the ACM*, 40(2):102–108 (February 1997), gives a concise overview of the history of the Internet, together with some speculations on future directions.

VIRTUAL COMMUNITIES AND OPEN SOURCE

Subhasish Dasgupta (ed.), *Encyclopedia of Virtual Communities and Technologies* (2005), is a comprehensive guide to designing, building, and living in virtual communities. Howard Rheingold, *The Virtual Community: Homesteading on the Electronic Frontier*, rev. ed. (2000), remarks on the transition of computer-mediated communication from an activity confined to enthusiasts to a growing aspect of popular culture.

J.C.R. Licklider and R.W. Taylor, "The Computer as a Communication Device," *Science and Technology* (April 1968), presents the authors' belief that computers and humans would soon come to think together in new ways. Stanley G. Smith and Bruce Arne Sherwood, "Educational Uses of the PLATO Computer System," *Science*, 192(4237):344–352 (April 1976), describes an early experiment with computer-mediated education. Howard Rheingold, *Tools for Thought: The History and Future of Mind-Amplifying Technology* (1985), includes interviews with some of the pioneers responsible for the creation of computer graphics, personal computers, and computer communication networks and looks forward to the use of modems to link individual computer users into networks and communities.

Yochai Benkler, *The Wealth of Networks: How Social Production Transforms Markets and Freedom* (2006), is a visionary tome on the power of networks. Barry Wellman, "Physical Place and Cyberplace: The Rise of Personalized Networking," *International Journal of Urban and Regional Research*, 25(2):227–252 (2001), discusses changes in the sense of community in the Internet age. Fred Turner, "Where the Counterculture Met the New Economy: The WELL and the Origins of Virtual Community," *Technology and Culture*, 46(3):485–512 (July 2005), describes what Stewart Brand, the communes of the 1960s, and the *Whole Earth Catalog* had to do with the origins of the Web.

Eric S. Raymond, *The Cathedral & the Bazaar*, rev. ed. (2001), collects various essays on the history and benefits of open source from one of its best-known advocates. Interesting accounts of the possible ramifications of collaborative social efforts over the Internet include Howard Rheingold, *Smart Mobs: The Next Social Revolution* (2002); Andrew Keen, *The Cult of the Amateur: How Today's Internet Is Killing Our Culture* (2007); David Weinberger, *Everything Is Miscellaneous: The Power of the New Digital Disorder* (2007); and Clay Shirky, *Here Comes Everybody: The Power of Organizing Without Organizations* (2008), and *Cognitive Surplus: Creativity and Generosity in a Connected Age* (2010).

The development of *Wikipedia* in particular is chronicled in Andrew Lih, *The Wikipedia Revolution: How a Bunch of Nobodies Created the World's Greatest Encyclopedia* (2009).

CYBERCRIME

Bruce Sterling, *The Hacker Crackdown: Law and Disorder on the Electronic Frontier* (1992), is an engaging and thoughtful discussion of the crackdown on hackers in the early 1990s.

Steven Levy, *Hackers: Heroes of the Computer Revolution*, updated ed. (2001), is an excellent introduction to hacker culture and computer security issues. Paul Mungo and Bryan Clough, *Approaching Zero* (1992), covers computer crime in Europe and the efforts of international police organizations to capture cybercriminals. John R. Vacca, *Identity Theft* (2003), by a retired computer security expert from NASA, explains steps to identify, investigate, and recover from identity theft. James R. Richards, *Transnational Criminal Organizations, Cybercrime, and Money Laundering* (1999), explains the workings of international criminal organizations, with particular emphasis on money laundering and wire fraud. Edward Waltz, *Information Warfare: Principles and Operations* (1998), details the potential threat to commercial, civil, and government information systems by belligerent states or organizations.

Other useful references on cybercrime include Bruce Schneier, *Secrets and Lies: Digital Security in a Networked World* (2000); Samuel C. McQuade III, *Understanding and Managing Cybercrime* (2006); Markus Jakobsson and Steven Myers (eds.), *Phishing and Countermeasures: Understanding the Increasing Problem of Electronic Identity Theft* (2007); J.M. Balkin et al. (eds.), *Cybercrime: Digital Cops in a Networked Environment* (2007); David S. Wall, *Cybercrime: The Transformation of Crime in the Information Age* (2007); Julie E. Mehan, *Cyberwar, Cyberterror, Cybercrime* (2008); Byron Acohido and Jon Swartz, *Zero Day Threat* (2008); Phillip Hallam-Baker, *The dotCrime Manifesto: How to Stop Internet Crime* (2008); and Markus Jakobsson and Zulfikar Ramzan, *Crimeware: Understanding New Attacks and Defenses* (2008).

DATA MINING AND PRIVACY

Bhavani Thuraisingham, *Data Mining: Technologies, Techniques, Tools, and Trends* (1999), gives an overview of data-mining technologies, applications, and the data-mining process. Jiawei Han and Micheline Kamber, *Data Mining: Concepts and Techniques*, 2nd ed. (2006), provides an introduction to the algorithms used in data mining and techniques for the development of those algorithms. Jaideep Vaidya, Chris Clifton, and Michael Zhu, *Privacy Preserving Data Mining* (2006), discusses privacy issues and methods for data mining that mitigate risks to privacy.

Daniel J. Solove, *The Digital Person: Technology and Privacy in the Information Age* (2004); and his *The Future of Reputation: Gossip, Rumor, and Privacy on the Internet* (2007), are wide-ranging discussions of the conflict between free speech and privacy over the Internet.

MEDIA CONVERGENCE

Chris Anderson, *The Long Tail: Why the Future of Business Is Selling Less of More* (2006), explores the proposition that, as the cost of distributing digitized books, music, films, and other content approaches zero, cultural consumption in the 21st century will be less constrained by the commercial need to market to mass tastes. Yochai Benkler, *The Wealth of Networks: How Social Production Transforms Markets and Freedom* (2006), argues that the rise of the Internet and the information economy has meant a growth in nonmarket or social forms of production and greater rewards for collaboration.

Brian Fitzgerald, "Creative Commons: Accessing, Negotiating, and Remixing Online Content," in Pandip Ninan Thomas and Jan Servaes (eds.), *Intellectual Property Rights and Communications in Asia* (2006), outlines the nature of creative commons and advocates its further development as a means of managing access to digital content for artists and creative producers.

Terry Flew, *Understanding Global Media* (2007), considers the impact of globalization and convergent technologies on various forms of media, and *New Media: An Introduction*, 2nd ed. (2005), provides an overview of key issues in the development of new media technologies and different academic approaches to understanding these developments. Lawrence Lessig, *Free Culture: How Big Media Uses Technology and the Law to Lock Down Culture and Control Creativity* (2004), using the example of open-source software development, argues that copyright and intellectual property laws should be less restrictive.

DISTANCE LEARNING

Books describing the use of specific technologies and pedagogical approaches include B.F. Skinner, *The Technology of Teaching* (1968); Alan Tait and Roger Mills (eds.), *The Convergence of Distance and Conventional Education: Patterns of Flexibility for the Individual Learner* (1999); Marc Eisenstadt and Tom Vincent, *The Knowledge Web: Learning and Collaborating on the Net* (1998); and A.W. (Tony) Bates, *Technology, E-Learning, and Distance Education*, 2nd ed. (2005). A wide range of books take up the controversial aspects of distance learning, including Thomas L. Russell (compiler), *The No Significant Difference Phenomenon* (1999); Gary A. Berg, *Why Distance Learning? Higher Education Administrative Practices* (2002); and David F. Noble, *Digital Diploma Mills: The Automation of Higher Education* (2001).

INDEX

04 12